SAGE Bookkeeper

SAGE
Bookkeeper

Training Guide

P. H. Bassett

Pitman

PITMAN PUBLISHING
128 Long Acre, London, WC2E 9AN

A Division of Longman Group UK Limited

© Paul Bassett 1989

First published in Great Britain 1989
Reprinted 1990

British Library Cataloguing in Publication Data
Bassett, P.H. (Paul Henry), *1954–*
    SAGE bookkeeper
    1. Accountancy. Applications of micro
    computer systems. Software packages. SAGE
    bookkeeper
    I. Title
    657.′028′553

ISBN 0-273-03053-1

Printed and bound in Singapore

Contents

Introduction

The purpose of this manual is primarily to assist students undertaking courses in Business and/or Computer Studies. A growing number of courses in these areas is now insisting that students have attained some skills in the use of new technology and business application packages.

A variety of reports has shown that accounts are the second most common business application of microcomputers (the most common being word processing applications). For this reason alone it is important that students should have the opportunity to use accounting packages as part of their course.

The use of accounts packages may also serve as an alternative means of instructing students in basic accounting principles.

The SAGE Bookkeeper package is widely used by small firms and as a simulated learning exercise for students using a 'beginners' accounts program. It is very simple to use and possesses many of the attributes that one would expect to find in a more expensive package. A large number of Colleges of Further Education have found that it is perfectly suited to the abilities and requirements of students on BTEC National level courses.

Whilst this manual is principally directed at students, it will also prove useful as a guide for the owners and managers of small firms who are using SAGE for their accounts. *Note:* the key words at the end of each task refer the user to other tasks where these words are used.

A wide range of 'IBM compatible' machines already exists, all of which are capable of running the SAGE Bookkeeper package. These machines come in a variety of different styles ranging from single drive to 40 megabyte hard disk systems.

Many educational establishments will also use different systems for ensuring the security of software, or alternatively systems designed to make access to software easier. This means that any instruction given in this manual as to the method of loading the SAGE package will invariably differ from the system set up in any particular college or by other users. Consequently, the space on the following page has deliberately been left to enable the user to enter the loading instructions that are specific to their own system.

SAGE is a registered trademark of SAGESOFT plc.

Twin disk drive

These computers have two floppy disk drives. One drive (referred to as drive A) is used for loading the program. The program disk is inserted in this drive and left there for the duration of the exercise.

The second drive (drive B) is used for the disk which contains the *data*. This means the information relating to the firm's accounts.

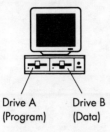

Drive A   Drive B
(Program) (Data)

Hard disk drive

This type of machine has only one disk drive, plus a hard disk. All of the programs should be stored on the hard disk. This means that to load a specific program you only have to type in the relevant instruction.

Data can be stored on the hard disk but this is not recommended in case the machine should 'crash'. Data is more often stored on a floppy disk which is loaded into the disk drive (usually referred to as drive A).

The hard disk is drive C and there will not normally be a drive B on this type of machine although most machines will assume that drive A is the same as drive B.

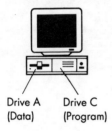

Drive A   Drive C
(Data)   (Program)

Instructions for loading SAGE bookkeeper

Switch the machine on and insert a system disk into drive A. When a > appears, place the SAGE disk into drive A and the DATA disk into drive B. Type SAGE and then press ENTER.

Switch the machine on. When a > prompt appears, place the DATA disk into drive A. Type SAGE and then press ENTER.

This space is left blank deliberately to enable users to enter their own loading instructions if an alternative to the above method is used.

Section A: Nominal Ledger ▬▬▬

Before using the SAGE package you will need a formatted floppy disk. Disks can be
formatted by selecting the appropriate option from the operating system.

Formatting is necessary to prepare a new blank disk for storing data and also to
erase all unwanted data from an existing disk.

If you are using other programs and already have data stored on your disk then you
will need to acquire a separate disk for use with the SAGE package, or delete any data
currently held on your disk.

Task 1   Loading SAGE

Objective

To load the SAGE program and set the correct date.

Instructions

Follow the instructions to load the SAGE program.

For the purposes of this and the following tasks the Dudley Trading Company will be
used throughout to highlight the features of the SAGE bookkeeper software package.
Enter the Company name as:

DUDLEY TRADING COMPANY
THE BROADWAY
DUDLEY
WEST MIDLANDS
DY1 4AA

You will then be asked to enter the date: enter the date as:

170987 ENTER

You will then be asked to enter the password, type:

LETMEIN ENTER

Note This will not appear on the screen.

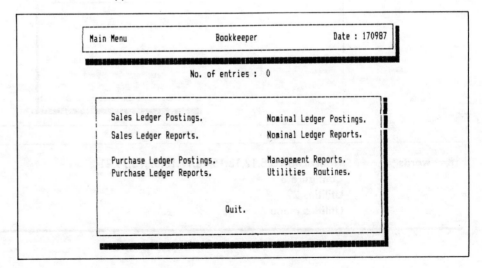

```
 Main Menu                 Bookkeeper              Date : 170987

                         No. of entries :  0


       Sales Ledger Postings.          Nominal Ledger Postings.
       Sales Ledger Reports.           Nominal Ledger Reports.

       Purchase Ledger Postings.       Management Reports.
       Purchase Ledger Reports.        Utilities  Routines.



                              Quit.

```

You should now insert your data disk into either drive A (hard disk machines) or drive B (twin drive machines).

The package will produce the screen display on p. 1.

SAGE is, like most accounting packages, a menu-driven package. This means that to select any command or function you simply select the required function from the menu by moving the cursor onto that function.

The cursor is moved by using the UP ↑ or DOWN ↓ ARROW keys until the cursor is positioned over the required function and then pressing the ENTER key.

Task 2

Configuring the package

Objective

To configure the package to suit Dudley Trading's requirements.

Instructions

Before any transaction data can be entered the package has to be 'configured' to suit the firm's specific requirements. This means that you will have to select how many accounts you will want in each ledger and also what reference numbers will be used for the different accounts.

Activity

You should now move the cursor onto the **UTILITIES ROUTINES** option and then press ENTER. This will produce the following **UTILITIES MENU**:

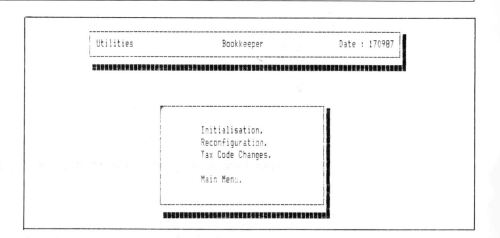

```
Utilities              Bookkeeper          Date : 170987
▪▪▪▪▪▪▪▪▪▪▪▪▪▪▪▪▪▪▪▪▪▪▪▪▪▪▪▪▪▪▪▪▪▪▪▪▪▪▪▪▪▪▪▪▪▪▪▪▪

              Initialisation,
              Reconfiguration,
              Tax Code Changes,

              Main Menu.

▪▪▪▪▪▪▪▪▪▪▪▪▪▪▪▪▪▪▪▪▪▪▪▪▪▪▪▪▪▪▪▪▪▪▪
```

Key words

Transaction 5,8,12,13,15,16,17,18,67,73,79,81
Configure 3
Utilities 29
Utilities menu 4

Task 3

Objective

Instructions

Configuring the system

To configure the package to specify the number and type of accounts required.

The options available are to set up the package for the accounts required (INITIALISATION), to amend account details already held (RECONFIGURATION), and to amend VAT rates (TAX CODE CHANGES). As the VAT rates have not been altered by the Government and there are no details to amend, the only suitable option is INITIALISATION. Move the cursor onto this item and press ENTER .

This function specifies how many accounts of each type will be required and also determines the Nominal Code numbers for the Control Accounts which are the most frequently used accounts.

Activity

Using this function will destroy any data already on disk and a warning is given on screen. As you have no data yet you can proceed. You will require 30 accounts in all three ledgers and the code numbers for the Control Accounts are as shown on the following screen. Enter these details as shown.

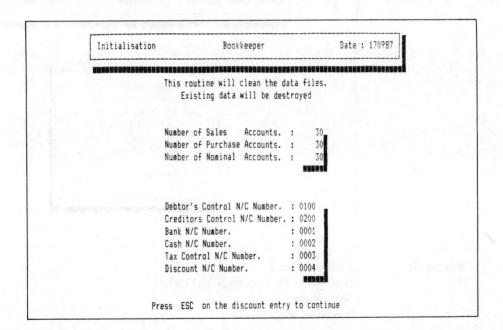

```
┌─────────────────────────────────────────────────────────────────┐
│ Initialisation          Bookkeeper            Date : 170987       │
│ ████████████████████████████████████████████████████████████████  │
│              This routine will clean the data files.              │
│              Existing data will be destroyed                      │
│                                                                   │
│                                                                   │
│           Number of Sales    Accounts. :     30                   │
│           Number of Purchase Accounts. :     30                   │
│           Number of Nominal  Accounts. :     30                   │
│                                                                   │
│                                                                   │
│                                                                   │
│           Debtor's Control N/C Number.  : 0100                    │
│           Creditors Control N/C Number. : 0200                    │
│           Bank N/C Number.              : 0001                    │
│           Cash N/C Number.              : 0002                    │
│           Tax Control N/C Number.       : 0003                    │
│           Discount N/C Number.          : 0004                    │
│                                                                   │
│        Press  ESC  on the discount entry to continue              │
└─────────────────────────────────────────────────────────────────┘
```

Key words

Initialise 29,50
(Re-)configure 2,40
Tax code 31

Task 4   **The nominal ledger menu**

Objective

To select the nominal ledger menu.

Instructions

When you have entered all the data you can, press ESC as instructed. The package will then save the account details onto your data disk, before returning to the UTILITIES MENU.

Activity

You can then select the option to return to the MAIN MENU and from that menu select the option for NOMINAL LEDGER POSTINGS. This will bring up the next menu.

As this is the first exercise it will be kept simple and you will only use the NOMINAL LEDGER part of the package. Future activities will examine the SALES and PURCHASE LEDGERS, and eventually you will use all of the ledgers together.

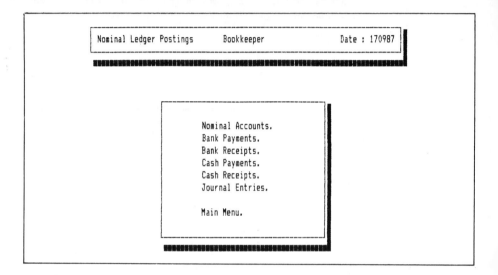

```
Nominal Ledger Postings      Bookkeeper          Date : 170987
████████████████████████████████████████████████████████████████


                     Nominal Accounts.
                     Bank Payments.
                     Bank Receipts.
                     Cash Payments.
                     Cash Receipts.
                     Journal Entries.

                     Main Menu.


               ████████████████████████████████████████
```

Key words

Utilities Menu 2
Nominal Ledger postings 30,31,37,42
Sales ledger
Purchases ledger

Task 5   Creating nominal accounts

Objective

To create accounts in the nominal ledger.

Instructions

You should now have the menu shown on the screen. You still cannot start to enter transaction details because you have not yet specified all of the accounts required. Before any transaction can be entered an account must first be created. Generally the firm will already have some idea of which accounts are needed (e.g. Sales, Purchases, Capital, Wages, etc) and these can be created straight away. Other accounts can always be created when needed. Your next step is to create the accounts that you will need in this section.

Activity

Select NOMINAL ACCOUNTS from the menu. You will then be asked to enter a reference number. *Note* Reference numbers must be different for each account and cannot be the same as those used for control accounts. Enter the reference number as 1000.

You will then be asked if this is a new account – N/Y – press **Y**. Next you will be asked for the account name – type SALES then press **ENTER**. The screen will clear to allow you to enter another reference number. Create the accounts as shown, all of which are new accounts; if you make a mistake use the cursor keys to make alterations.

2000	PURCHASES
3000	CAPITAL
4000	WAGES
4100	RENT
4200	RATES
4300	LIGHT & HEAT
4400	INSURANCE
4500	MOTOR EXPENSES
5000	FIXTURES
6000	MOTOR VEHICLES

Key words

Transaction 2,8,12,13,15,16,17,28,67,73,79,81
Nominal accounts 30,56
Control accounts 17,23,24,25,30

Task 6   **Selecting bank receipts**

Objective

To select the option for entering details of bank receipts.

Instructions

When you have finished you need to return to the NOMINAL POSTINGS menu. To do this press ESC.

Activity

You can now start to enter some data. The first transaction is that the owner of Dudley Trading has invested capital into a bank account of £10,000. To enter this transaction select BANK RECEIPTS from the menu.

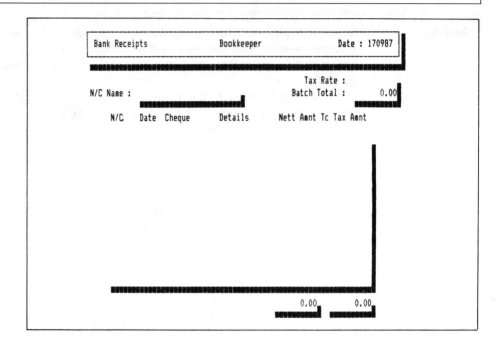

Key words

Bank receipts 7,8,9,11,16,32
Nominal postings 9,11,12,14,15,17

Task 7   Entering bank receipts

Objective

To enter details of bank receipts.

Instructions

You should have the above screen and the cursor should be flashing under N/C – check that it is the BANK RECEIPTS screen! Type in 3000 as the N/C and the word CAPITAL should then appear as N/C Name (the reference number for capital is 3000).

All accounts in the nominal ledger have to be given a number, when this number is typed in Sage will automatically enter the account name. The term N/C is an abbreviation for Nominal Code; in the Sales and Purchase ledgers, numbers and letters can be used for Account Codes and the abbreviation in those ledgers is A/C.

Activity

The cursor will automatically move to DATE – you could retype this but if the transaction occurs on the date in the top left of the screen then this can be copied by pressing the **F1** key. Do this now.

The REF: is used to give details of the invoice or cheque number used in a transaction; enter the cheque number as 230987. DETAILS can be used for a short description of transactions – you can enter Opening Capital. NETT AMNT is for recording the amount received which in this case is 10,000. TC refers to the VAT code and a code has to be entered – the only codes currently used are T0 – no VAT and T1 – VAT at 15%. Type T0 for no VAT. TAX AMNT is only used if there is any VAT and will automatically calculate VAT payable.

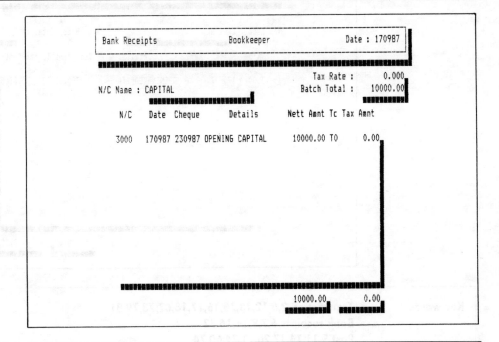

```
Bank Receipts            Bookkeeper           Date : 170987

                                      Tax Rate :      0.000
N/C Name : CAPITAL                    Batch Total :  10000.00

    N/C    Date  Cheque     Details      Nett Amnt Tc Tax Amnt

   3000  170987 230987 OPENING CAPITAL   10000.00 T0     0.00




                                         10000.00         0.00
```

Key words   Bank receipts 6,8,9,11,16,32

Task 8

Posting Transactions

Objective

To post (save) transactions that have been entered correctly.

Instructions

This is the only transaction involving BANK RECEIPTS at the moment so you need to save this transaction and move onto another item. SAGE will assume that you are posting more than one item at a time and will be waiting for you to enter the next line. To exit this screen you will have to press `ESC`; SAGE will then ask if you want to POST, EDIT or ABANDON the transaction. You want to POST (i.e. save) the transaction and as this is the item highlighted you can simply press `ENTER`. SAGE will then save the transaction details before returning to the BANK RECEIPTS screen. To exit this screen press `ESC` again.

Activity

The owner of Dudley Trading has also invested capital in cash to the value of £300.00 on the same day. Select the CASH RECEIPTS option and see if you can enter the transaction details – remember `F1` will copy the date.

When you have finished the screen should look like this:

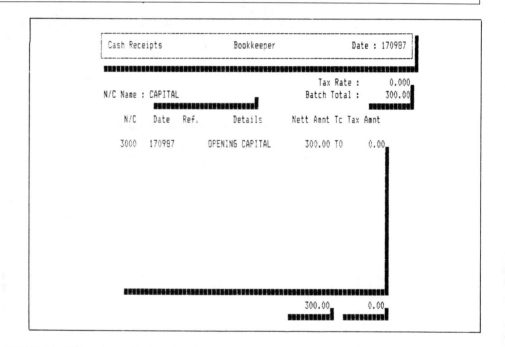

Key words

Transaction 2,5,12,13,15,16,17,18,67,73,79,81
Bank receipts 6,7,9,11,16,32
Post 9,11,14,17,20,21,34,60,74
Edit 9,38,39
Abandon 9
Posting transactions 9,68
Cash receipts 14,35

Task 9

Rectifying errors

Objective

To rectify errors if incorrect entries have been made.

Instructions

If you have made any errors, they can be rectified by moving the cursor back with the cursor keys and overtyping any error.

Activity

Move the cursor back to the Details column and type OPENING BALANCE. This should over-type the existing entry. Entries in any of the columns can be altered by overtyping in this way. Now press `ESC` and the prompt will ask if you want to Post, Edit or Abandon. If the entry was a complete mess you could move the cursor to Abandon and then press `ENTER`. Instead move the cursor to Edit and press `ENTER` The cursor will move back into the top part of the screen and you can edit in the same way as described above. Move the cursor back to the Details field and change the entry back to OPENING CAPITAL.

Once you have done this press `ESC`, select Post to post the transaction, and return to the NOMINAL POSTINGS menu.

Key words

Opening Balance 31,54,67
Post 8,11,14,17,20,21,34,60,74
Edit 8,38,39
Abandon 8
Bank receipts 6,7,8,11,16,32
Nominal postings 6,11,12,14,15,17
Posting transactions 8,68

Note If you are unable to complete a section within the time available, make a note as to how far you had got, and exit the program by carefully working your way back through the menus to the MAIN MENU and then select QUIT. Failure to exit properly can result in your data being corrupted.

Task 10   **Entering bank payments**

Objective   To enter details of bank payments.

Instructions   The next thing that Dudley Trading does is to buy some stock using the money in the bank account. To enter these select BANK PAYMENTS from the menu.

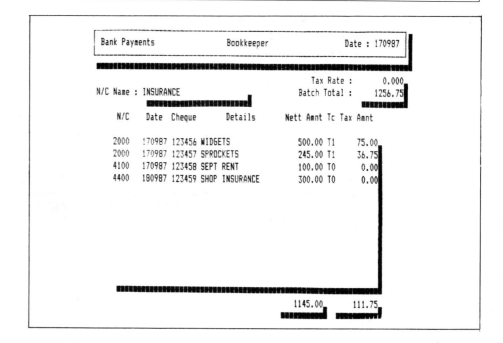

N/C	Date	Cheque	Details	Nett Amnt	Tc	Tax Amnt
2000	170987	123456	WIDGETS	500.00	T1	75.00
2000	170987	123457	SPROCKETS	245.00	T1	36.75
4100	170987	123458	SEPT RENT	100.00	T0	0.00
4400	180987	123459	SHOP INSURANCE	300.00	T0	0.00
				1145.00		111.75

Bank Payments — Bookkeeper — Date : 170987
Tax Rate : 0.000
N/C Name : INSURANCE — Batch Total : 1256.75

Key words   Bank payments 11,33

Task 11   **Posting instructions**

Objective

To post (save) transactions and exit the program.

Instructions

When you have entered these items press `ESC`, then select POST and when the screen reappears press `ESC` to return to the NOMINAL POSTINGS menu.

This ends the first section, which has demonstrated how to create accounts and record bank payments and receipts. You can either finish now or continue with section B. Provided that you retain your disk it should be possible to stop and start lessons at any point.

Activity

To exit the program properly and safeguard your data you should first select MAIN MENU. When you have returned to the MAIN MENU select QUIT and do not remove your disk until the opening screen prompt reappears. Retain your data disk for Section B.

Key words

Post 8,9,14,17,20,21,34,60,74
Nominal postings 6,9,12,14,15,17
Bank payments 10,33
Bank receipts 6,7,8,9,16,32
Quit

Section B: Nominal Ledger ▬▬▬▬▬▬

Task 12

The function keys

Objective

To use the function **F** keys to simplify data entry.

Instructions

Section A demonstrated how to create accounts and record bank payments and receipts. Examine some of the other options available in the nominal ledger such as credit transactions and cash receipts/payments.

When entering transaction details the following function keys are available:
F1 copies date from top left of screen
F2 copies data from previous line
F3 sets Tax code as T1 (VAT=15%)

If you have not already loaded SAGE do so now and set the date as 170987. Remember, the password is LETMEIN.

Activity

Select NOMINAL POSTINGS from the menu.

The owner of Dudley Trading has now acquired a motor vehicle on credit terms from ABC Motors for £5,500. As no payment has yet been made in cash or by cheque, this cannot be recorded under BANK or CASH. The only remaining option is JOURNAL ENTRIES – select this option now.

The journal is a temporary store of transactions that have been made, and which can be checked before they are entered in the final accounts

Set the date at 170987 by pressing **F1** and enter the reference as dct1. The entries in the journal require a knowledge of double-entry bookkeeping principles and for every transaction two accounts must be adjusted. *Note* there is a warning on the screen that the batch total must equal *zero* before exit – this means that the debit column must be exactly the same total as the credit column.

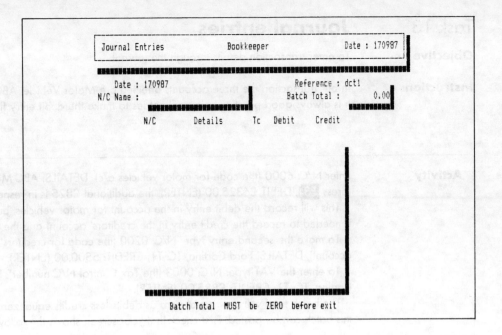

```
┌─────────────────────────────────────────────────────────────┐
│                                                             │
│   Journal Entries              Bookkeeper        Date : 170987 │
│   ████████████████████████████████████████████████████████  │
│     Date : 170987                    Reference : dct1        │
│     N/C Name :                       Batch Total :      0.00 │
│     ████████████████████████         █████████              │
│       N/C      Details      Tc   Debit      Credit          │
│                                                             │
│                                                             │
│                                                             │
│                                                             │
│                                                             │
│     ████████████████████████████████████████████            │
│              Batch Total  MUST  be  ZERO  before exit       │
│                                                             │
└─────────────────────────────────────────────────────────────┘
```

Key words	Function keys 32,55
	Nominal postings 6,9,11,14,15,17
	Journal 24,31
	Journal entries 13,14,19,20,37,42
	Transaction 2,5,8,13,15,16,17,18,67,73,79,81

Task 13   **Journal entries**

Objective

To enter transaction details through the journal.

Instructions

In our transaction the three accounts affected are Motor Vehicle, ABC Motors and VAT. It is always good practice in journal entries to make the debit entry first.

Activity

Enter N/C: 6000 (the code for motor vehicles a/c), DETAILS: ABC Motors, TC: T1 (press **F3**), DEBIT £6325.00 (ENTER), the additional £825 is in respect of VAT.

This will record the debit entry in the account for motor vehicles, but another entry is needed to record the credit entry in the creditors' account and the VAT.

To make the second entry type: N/C: 0200 (the code for creditors' control account), DETAILS: Ford Cortina, TC: T1, CREDIT: 5500.00 (ENTER).

To enter the VAT type: N/C: 0003 (the Tax Control N/C number), DETAILS: Ford Cortina, TC: T1, CREDIT: £825.00 (ENTER).

The batch total will now equal *zero* as debits less credits equal zero, and therefore this batch can be posted. First check that your screen shows the following:

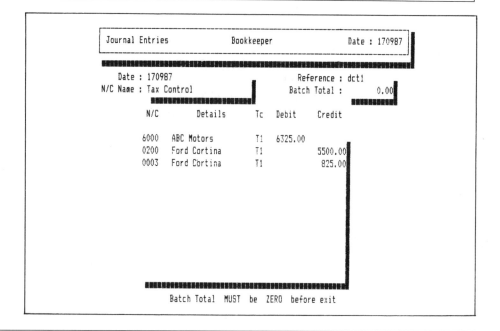

```
 ┌─────────────────────────────────────────────────────────────┐
 │  Journal Entries           Bookkeeper           Date : 170987 │
 └─────────────────────────────────────────────────────────────┘
 ████████████████████████████████████████████████████████████████

        Date : 170987                    Reference : dct1
   N/C Name : Tax Control                Batch Total :        0.00
        ███████████████████████                      ████████████

          N/C       Details      Tc   Debit      Credit

          6000    ABC Motors     T1   6325.00
          0200    Ford Cortina   T1              5500.00
          0003    Ford Cortina   T1               825.00


 ████████████████████████████████████████████████████████████████
              Batch Total  MUST  be  ZERO  before exit
```

Key words

Journal entries 12,14,19,20,37,42
Transaction 2,5,8,12,15,16,17,18,67,73,79,81

Task 14

Entering cash receipts.

Objective

To select the cash receipts option and enter details of cash receipts.

Instructions

Journal entries can be posted in the usual way by first pressing **ESC**, then selecting POST. This will return you to journal entries. As there are no more journal entries at the moment you can press **ESC** to return to the NOMINAL POSTINGS menu.

Activity

Dudley Trading has now sold some of the stock for cash and therefore some entries are needed under CASH RECEIPTS. Select this item from the menu and record the following transactions — remember that the function keys **F1** (date), **F2** (previous line) and **F3** (Tax Code 1) are available to assist you.

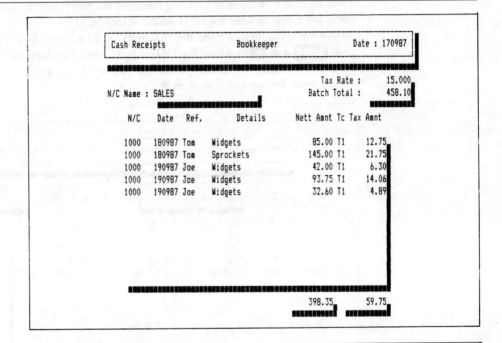

```
Cash Receipts              Bookkeeper              Date : 170987


                                               Tax Rate :      15.000
N/C Name : SALES                               Batch Total :   458.10


      N/C    Date    Ref.       Details      Nett Amnt Tc Tax Amnt

      1000   180987  Tom     Widgets            85.00  T1   12.75
      1000   180987  Tom     Sprockets         145.00  T1   21.75
      1000   190987  Joe     Widgets            42.00  T1    6.30
      1000   190987  Joe     Widgets            93.75  T1   14.06
      1000   190987  Joe     Widgets            32.60  T1    4.89




                                               398.35       59.75
```

Key words

Journal entries 12,13,19,20,37,42
Post 8,9,11,17,20,21,34,60,74
Nominal postings 6,9,11,12,15,17
Cash receipts 8,35

Task 15   **Entering cash payments**

Objective

To enter details of cash payments and calculate VAT where tax is inclusive of the price.

Instructions

When you have entered these transactions, post them and then press <kbd>ESC</kbd> to return to the NOMINAL POSTINGS menu.

The owner has also had to make some payments for expense items in cash. Select CASH PAYMENTS to record these items. The expenses that he has paid are: petrol £10.00, wages £75.00 and electricity £35.00.

Activity

The first item to record is the petrol; this will be entered in the account for motor expenses (N/C: 4500). Enter 4500 as the code and the date as 200987. Use car as the REF and Petrol as the DETAILS. The NETT AMNT can be entered as £10.00.

This amount is *inclusive* of VAT and therefore the NETT AMT should be less — SAGE will calculate what the NETT AMNT is for you.

Enter the tax code as T1 and the TAX AMNT will be shown as £1.50. Now press <kbd>SHIFT</kbd> and <kbd><</kbd> together. The NETT AMNT and TAX AMNT will recalculate to show £8.70 and £1.30. SAGE has worked out the VAT for you.

Now enter the remaining items as shown.

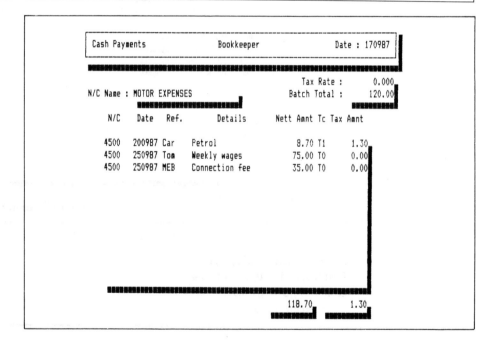

```
┌─────────────────────────────────────────────────────────────┐
│ Cash Payments            Bookkeeper          Date : 170987    │
└─────────────────────────────────────────────────────────────┘

                                       Tax Rate :       0.000
  N/C Name : MOTOR EXPENSES            Batch Total :    120.00

      N/C    Date    Ref.      Details        Nett Amnt Tc Tax Amnt

      4500   200987 Car      Petrol               8.70 T1     1.30
      4500   250987 Tom      Weekly wages        75.00 T0     0.00
      4500   250987 MEB      Connection fee      35.00 T0     0.00




                                               118.70          1.30
```

Key words

Transaction 2,5,8,12,13,16,17,67,73,79,81
Nominal postings 6,9,11,12,14,17
Cash payments 16,36

Task 16   Entering bank receipts

Objective

To enter bank receipts in respect of sales.

Instructions

There are several more transactions that take place before the end of the month and the first batch involves BANK RECEIPTS. Post the CASH PAYMENTS and select BANK RECEIPTS once more.

Activity

Dudley Trading has received a number of cheques as payment for sales. Enter the details shown on the following screen. All items are to be entered in N/C 1000 (the code for sales).

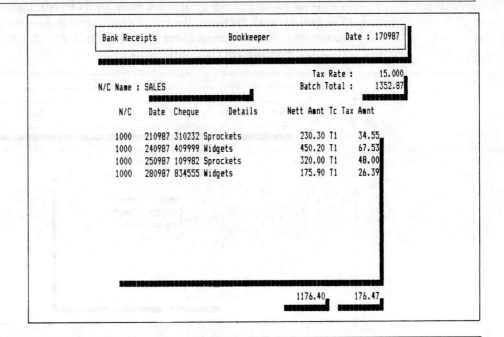

```
Bank Receipts              Bookkeeper           Date : 170987
■■■■■■■■■■■■■■■■■■■■■■■■■■■■■■■■■■■■■■■■■■■■■

                                        Tax Rate :      15.000
   N/C Name : SALES                     Batch Total :   1352.87
   ■■■■■■■■■■■■■■■■■■■■■■■■■

      N/C   Date   Cheque    Details    Nett Amnt Tc Tax Amnt

      1000  210987 310232 Sprockets       230.30 T1    34.55
      1000  240987 409999 Widgets         450.20 T1    67.53
      1000  250987 109982 Sprockets       320.00 T1    48.00
      1000  280987 834555 Widgets         175.90 T1    26.39




   ■■■■■■■■■■■■■■■■■■■■■■■■■■■■■■■■■■■■■■■■■■
                                       1176.40      176.47
```

Key words

Transaction 2,5,8,12,13,15,17,18,67,73,79,81
Bank receipts 6,7,8,9,11,32
Cash payments 15,36

Examining the cash account

Objective   To transfer cash takings to the bank account.

Instructions   When you have entered the details shown, POST these transactions and then press `ESC` to return to the NOMINAL POSTINGS menu — remember that mistakes can be rectified using the cursor keys.

There will be occasions when the owner of a business will decide that cash takings need to be 'banked'. This will usually be done on a daily basis or whenever cash in hand exceeds a set figure. For the purposes of this task it will be necessary to examine the cash account to see how much cash is in the 'till'.

Activity   To examine the cash account, first return to the MAIN MENU. Then select NOMINAL LEDGER REPORTS. The cash account is one of the more important accounts and therefore can be found under CONTROL ACCOUNTS — select this option, and then select PETTY CASH.

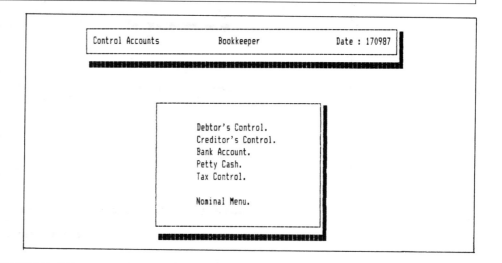

```
Control Accounts          Bookkeeper          Date : 170987
████████████████████████████████████████████████████████████

                    Debtor's Control.
                    Creditor's Control.
                    Bank Account.
                    Petty Cash.
                    Tax Control.

                    Nominal Menu.

             ███████████████████████████████████████
```

Key words   Post 8,9,11,14,20,21,34,60,74
Transactions 2,5,8,12,13,15,16,18,67,73,79,81
Nominal postings 6,9,11,12,14,15
Nominal ledger reports 21,38,39
Control accounts 5,23,24,25,30
Petty cash

Task 18   Examining the petty cash

Objective   To examine the petty cash account.

Instructions   This part of the program has been set up to allow you to examine selected parts of the required account and consequently you will now be asked to identify which transactions you want to examine. You want to see all transactions so press ENTER as the response to the queries:

Lower transaction No: ENTER
Upper transaction No: ENTER

Activity   The next option to decide is where you want the response to be sent – the options are Display (i.e.: the screen), Printer or File. As you only want to check the balance of the account you should select DISP.

You should then have the following screen display:

```
┌─────────────────────────────────────────────────────────────────────┐
│  Petty Cash                Bookkeeper               Date : 170987     │
│  ██████████████████████████████████████████████████████████████████  │
│                                                                        │
│  A/C Ref. : 0002                      A/C Name : Cash                 │
│         █████                            ████████████████████████     │
│                                                                        │
│  No. Tp  Date   Ref      Details       Value      Debit     Credit    │
│                                                                        │
│    2 CR 170987          OPENING CAPITAL  300.00    300.00             │
│   10 CR 180987 Tom      Widgets           97.75                       │
│   11 CR 180987 Tom      Sprockets        166.75    264.50             │
│   12 CR 190987 Joe      Widgets           48.30                       │
│   13 CR 190987 Joe      Widgets          107.81                       │
│   14 CR 190987 Joe      Widgets           37.49    193.60             │
│   15 CP 200987 Car      Petrol            10.00               10.00   │
│   16 CP 250987 Tom      Weekly wages      75.00               75.00   │
│   17 CP 250987 MEB      Connection fee    35.00               35.00   │
│                                                                        │
│  ██████████████████████████████████████████████████████████████████  │
│                                        Totals  :   758.10    120.00   │
│                                        Balance :   638.10             │
│                                                  ██████████████████    │
│              Press  ESC  to finish,  RETURN to continue               │
└─────────────────────────────────────────────────────────────────────┘
```

Key words   **Transaction 2,5,8,12,13,15,16,17,67,73,79,81**

Task 19   **Making 'contra' entries**

Objective

To make a 'contra' entry from the cash account to the bank account using the journal.

Instructions

The balance currently available in the 'till' is £638.10. This is more than is needed so you can transfer £500 into the bank account.

As this transaction involves both bank and cash accounts it will have to be entered by making a journal entry. Press <kbd>ESC</kbd> to leave the petty cash screen display.

Contra entries are made when an amount is transferred from one account where it is entered as a debit, to another account where it is entered as a credit, thereby being entered twice.

Activity

Select JOURNAL ENTRIES, and then enter the transfer of £500 to the bank account (debit) from the cash account (credit). The N/C codes are Bank 0001 and Cash 0002; set the date as 250987. Do not worry if you make any mistakes as these can be corrected later.

You should have the following if you have entered the transaction correctly.

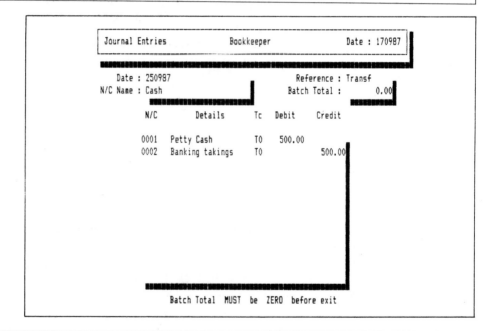

```
Journal Entries              Bookkeeper              Date : 170987
████████████████████████████████████████████████████████████████

    Date : 250987                        Reference : Transf
N/C Name : Cash                          Batch Total :        0.00

         N/C        Details      Tc   Debit     Credit

         0001    Petty Cash      T0   500.00
         0002    Banking takings T0             500.00




               Batch Total  MUST  be  ZERO  before exit
```

Key words

Journal entries 12,13,14,20,37,42
Contra entries

Journal entries

Objective

To enter details of fixed assets bought on credit using the journal.

Instructions

Do not POST these items yet as there are some more journal entries to be made. Enter these items as journal entries — the N/C codes are given in brackets.

Activity

The owner bought some shop fittings (5000) for £2,000 from Dudley Fitters (0200) on 25 Sept 1987. VAT is payable at the standard rate.

He also sold some sprockets (1000) on credit to XYZ Ltd (0100) for £300.00 on the same day — VAT 15%.

Your screen should show the following; if you have entered the debits/credits on the wrong side then adjust your entries now.

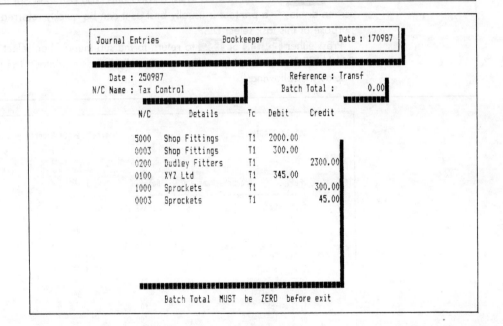

```
Journal Entries              Bookkeeper              Date : 170987

      Date : 250987                        Reference : Transf
  N/C Name : Tax Control                   Batch Total :        0.00

          N/C       Details      Tc   Debit       Credit

          5000   Shop Fittings   T1   2000.00
          0003   Shop Fittings   T1    300.00
          0200   Dudley Fitters  T1                2300.00
          0100   XYZ Ltd         T1    345.00
          1000   Sprockets       T1                 300.00
          0003   Sprockets       T1                  45.00




                  Batch Total  MUST  be  ZERO  before exit
```

Key words

Post 8,9,11,14,17,21,34,60,74
Journal entries 12,13,14,19,37,42

Task 21   **Examining account names**

Objective   To obtain details of all account names currently in use.

Instructions   The owner of Dudley Trading has no further transactions to be entered for this month but would like to examine his financial position at the month-end.

POST the journal entries and return to the MAIN MENU. Then select NOMINAL LEDGER REPORTS.

Activity

The first of the new options is ACCOUNT NAMES, this option will display or print out the names and numbers given to accounts. It is useful when a large number of accounts are used as it is very easy to forget infrequently used codes.

You will be asked to specify which account references are to be listed. Press ENTER for both queries to list all accounts. You can then opt for a printout or screen display – a printout is usually best as it can be quickly referred to, but for the purpose of this task select DISP.

Press either ENTER or ESC to return to the sub-menu. Then select TRIAL BALANCE. You can opt for either a screen display or a printout. The printout should display the following:

```
      DUDLEY TRADING PLC                     Nominal Ledger Reports - Trial Balance.


          Ref.      Accounts Name      Debit       Credit
          ------    -----------------  ----------  ----------
          0001    Bank                 10596.12
          0002    Cash                   138.10
          0003    Tax Control                         693.17
          0100    Debtor's Control       345.00
          0200    Creditors Control                  7800.00
          1000    SALES                              1874.75
          2000    PURCHASES              745.00
          3000    CAPITAL                           10300.00
          4100    RENT                   100.00
          4400    INSURANCE              300.00
          4500    MOTOR EXPENSES         118.70
          5000    FIXTURES              2000.00
          6000    MOTOR VEHICLES        6325.00
                                       ----------  ----------
                                        20667.92    20667.92
```

Key words   **Post** 8,9,11,14,17,20,34,60,74
Nominal ledger reports 17,38,39
Account names 37
Trial balance 39

Task 22

Account history reports

Objective

To obtain a history of any accounts transactions.

Instructions

The next option is for the QUICK RATIO. At present this option will not do anything as it has not yet been set up and will therefore be left for a later task.

Activity

ACCOUNT HISTORY will produce a report showing all the activity in any of the accounts selected. Once again you can request a specific range of accounts. *Do not request a printout of all accounts as this will waste paper:* accounts can and should be examined on screen. However, if you really need a printout then you can reselect the option and specify one account only.

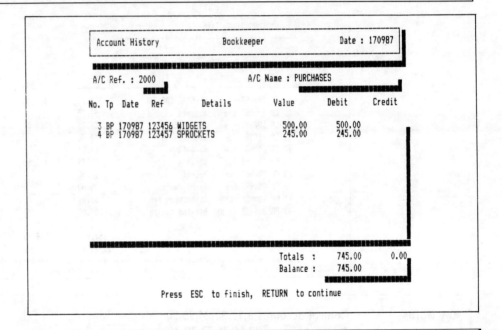

```
Account History            Bookkeeper              Date : 170987

A/C Ref. : 2000                      A/C Name : PURCHASES

No. Tp Date   Ref      Details          Value     Debit    Credit

  3 BP 170987 123456 WIDGETS           500.00    500.00
  4 BP 170987 123457 SPROCKETS         245.00    245.00




                                    Totals :    745.00      0.00
                                    Balance :   745.00

        Press  ESC  to finish,  RETURN  to continue
```

Key words

Quick ratio 38,39
Account history 23,66,76,77,78,79

Task 23   **Examining control accounts**

Objective   To obtain a history of the transactions in the cash or bank account.

Instructions   The ACCOUNT HISTORY will not provide details of the CONTROL ACCOUNTS: these are selected separately.

Activity   Select the CASH account and request all transactions to be included. If you print this out you will obtain the following screen:

```
    DUDLEY TRADING PLC                    Control Accounts - Petty Cash.


    Account : 0002    Cash
    -------------------------------------------------


    No. Tp Date   Ref       Details        Value      Debit      Credit
    ==== == ====== ====== ==================== ========== ========== ==========
      2 CR 170987           OPENING CAPITAL    300.00     300.00
     10 CR 180987 Tom       Widgets            97.75
     11 CR 180987 Tom       Sprockets         166.75     264.50
     12 CR 190987 Joe       Widgets            48.30
     13 CR 190987 Joe       Widgets           107.81
     14 CR 190987 Joe       Widgets            37.49     193.60
     15 CP 200987 Car       Petrol             10.00                 10.00
     16 CP 250987 Tom       Weekly wages       75.00                 75.00
     17 CP 250987 MEB       Connection fee     35.00                 35.00
     23 JC 250987 Transf    Banking takings   500.00                500.00

                                       Totals  :      758.10    620.00
                                       Balance :      138.10
    ==============================================================================
```

Key words   Control accounts 5,17,23,24,25,30
Account history 22,66,76,77,78,79

Task 24

Interpreting entries

Objective

To interpret the entries made and to obtain management reports, including daybooks.

Instructions

The control accounts are set out in the same way as the ordinary accounts and record:

No.	transaction number
Tp	transaction type
N/C	Nominal Code of other account involved
Date	transaction date
Ref	reference used for transaction
Details	details used for transaction
Value	entered as debit or credit

The transaction types used throughout the system are:

Credits		Debits	
SI	Sales invoice	PI	Purchase invoice
PC	Purchase credit note	SC	Sales credit note
BR	Bank receipt	BP	Bank payment
CR	Cash receipt	CP	Cash payment
JC	Journal credit	JD	Journal Debit

SAGE can also provide management reports: return to the MAIN MENU and then select MANAGEMENT REPORTS.

Activity

The option for DAYBOOKS is primarily included for use with the Sales and Purchase Ledgers and accordingly will only produce details from the journal. Select this option if required to obtain the following screen/printout:

```
DUDLEY TRADING PLC                     Day Books - Journal Entries.


No. Tp  A/C   N/C    Date   Ref.      Details        Debit      Credit
---- -- ----- ------ ------ ------   --------------  ----------  ----------
   7 JD        6000  170987 dct1     ABC Motors       6325.00
   8 JC        0200  170987 dct1     Ford Cortina                  5500.00
   9 JC        0003  170987 dct1     Ford Cortina                   825.00
  22 JD        0001  250987 Transf   Petty Cash        500.00
  23 JC        0002  250987 Transf   Banking takings                500.00
  24 JD        5000  250987 Transf   Shop Fittings    2000.00
  25 JD        0003  250987 Transf   Shop Fittings     300.00
  26 JC        0200  250987 Transf   Dudley Fitters                2300.00
  27 JD        0100  250987 Transf   XYZ Ltd           345.00
  28 JC        1000  250987 Transf   Sprockets                      300.00
  29 JC        0003  250987 Transf   Sprockets                       45.00
                                                     ----------  ----------
                                                      9470.00     9470.00
```

Key words

Control accounts 5,17,23,24,30
Reference codes
Management reports 40,43,63,64
Daybooks 63,81
Journal 12,31

Task 25

Examining the audit trail

Objective

To print out and examine the audit trail.

Instructions

The next option is the AUDIT TRAIL, this is important as it gives details of every transaction and will appear in the same order as details have been entered. It should be retained as it is vital proof that transactions have taken place.

Activity

Select this option and press `ENTER` to accept the DEFAULT VALUES, but ask for a printout as the AUDIT TRAIL is not very clear on screen.

Most of the details shown are similar to those in other printouts. N–AC is used only in the sales and purchase ledgers but has the same purpose as N–NC in that it shows the next transaction in the same account. Note that transaction no 8 has an N–NC entry of 24. This is because no 24 is the next entry in nominal code 0200. The N–NC entry is only used for CONTROL ACCOUNTS.

```
DUDLEY TRADING PLC                      Management Reports - Audit Trail.                                    Date : 170987
                                                                                                             Page :    1

No. Type A/C   N/C   Details         Date    Inv.  Nett Amount Tax Amount  TC  Paid  Date   Cheque Amount Paid  N-AC  N-NC
---- ----  ------  ------  --------------- ------  ------  ----------- ----------- ---  ----  ------  -------- ------------  ----  ----
  1  BR    3000   OPENING CAPITAL   170987 230987    10000.00      0.00  T0   Y   170987 230987      10000.00    0     2
  2  CR    3000   OPENING CAPITAL   170987               300.00      0.00  T0   Y   170987               300.00    0     0
  3  BP    2000   WIDGETS           170987 123456      500.00     75.00  T1   Y   170987 123456        575.00    0     4
  4  BP    2000   SPROCKETS         170987 123457      245.00     36.75  T1   Y   170987 123457        281.75    0     0
  5  BP    4100   SEPT RENT         170987 123458      100.00      0.00  T0   Y   170987 123458        100.00    0     0
  6  BP    4400   SHOP INSURANCE    180987 123459      300.00      0.00  T0   Y   180987 123459        300.00    0     0
  7  JD    6000   ABC Motors        170987 dct1       6325.00      0.00  T1   Y   170987 dct1         6325.00    0     0
  8  JC    0200   Ford Cortina      170987 dct1       5500.00      0.00  T1   Y   170987 dct1         5500.00    0    26
  9  JC    0003   Ford Cortina      170987 dct1        825.00      0.00  T1   Y   170987 dct1          825.00    0    25
 10  CR    1000   Widgets           180987 Tom          85.00     12.75  T1   Y   180987 Tom            97.75    0    11
 11  CR    1000   Sprockets         180987 Tom         145.00     21.75  T1   Y   180987 Tom           166.75    0    12
 12  CR    1000   Widgets           190987 Joe          42.00      6.30  T1   Y   190987 Joe            48.30    0    13
 13  CR    1000   Widgets           190987 Joe          93.75     14.06  T1   Y   190987 Joe           107.81    0    14
 14  CR    1000   Widgets           190987 Joe          32.60      4.89  T1   Y   190987 Joe            37.49    0    18
 15  CP    4500   Petrol            200987 Car           8.70      1.30  T1   Y   200987 Car            10.00    0    16
 16  CP    4500   Weekly wages      250987 Tom          75.00      0.00  T0   Y   250987 Tom            75.00    0    17
 17  CP    4500   Connection fee    250987 MEB          35.00      0.00  T0   Y   250987 MEB            35.00    0     0
 18  BR    1000   Sprockets         210987 310232      230.30     34.55  T1   Y   210987 310232        264.85    0    19
 19  BR    1000   Widgets           240987 409999      450.20     67.53  T1   Y   240987 409999        517.73    0    20
 20  BR    1000   Sprockets         250987 109982      320.00     48.00  T1   Y   250987 109982        368.00    0    21
 21  BR    1000   Widgets           280987 834555      175.90     26.39  T1   Y   280987 834555        202.29    0    28
 22  JD    0001   Petty Cash        250987 Transf       500.00      0.00  T0   Y   250987 Transf        500.00    0     0
 23  JC    0002   Banking takings   250987 Transf       500.00      0.00  T0   Y   250987 Transf        500.00    0     0
 24  JD    5000   Shop Fittings     250987 Transf      2000.00      0.00  T1   Y   250987 Transf       2000.00    0     0
 25  JD    0003   Shop Fittings     250987 Transf       300.00      0.00  T1   Y   250987 Transf        300.00    0    29
 26  JC    0200   Dudley Fitters    250987 Transf      2300.00      0.00  T1   Y   250987 Transf       2300.00    0     0
 27  JD    0100   XYZ Ltd           250987 Transf       345.00      0.00  T1   Y   250987 Transf        345.00    0     0
 28  JC    1000   Sprockets         250987 Transf       300.00      0.00  T1   Y   250987 Transf        300.00    0     0
 29  JC    0003   Sprockets         250987 Transf        45.00      0.00  T1   Y   250987 Transf         45.00    0     0
```

Key words

Audit trail 64
Control accounts 5,17,23,24,30
Default values

Task 26 VAT returns

Objective   To obtain a VAT return.

Instructions   The VAT RETURN option categorises VAT between the different rates and Ledgers. As you have only used two rates (nil and 15%) and only one ledger, there is no point in examining this item at the moment.

Activity   The report that the owner will almost certainly want is the next item, MONTHLY ACCOUNTS. Select this and then select the PROFIT & LOSS option. You should then obtain the following screen:

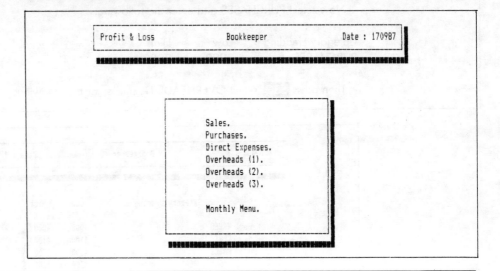

```
┌──────────────────────────────────────────────────────────┐
│ Profit & Loss          Bookkeeper          Date : 170987  │
└──────────────────────────────────────────────────────────┘
 ████████████████████████████████████████████████████████████

                    ┌──────────────────────────┐
                    │                          │
                    │   Sales.                 │
                    │   Purchases.             │
                    │   Direct Expenses.       │
                    │   Overheads (1).         │
                    │   Overheads (2).         │
                    │   Overheads (3).         │
                    │                          │
                    │   Monthly Menu.          │
                    │                          │
                    └──────────────────────────┘
           ████████████████████████████████████████
```

Key words   **VAT returns**
Monthly accounts 27,40,41
Profit and Loss accounts 28,31,40,41,43

Task 27   Designing the profit and loss account

Objective

To select the contents required in the profit and loss account.

Instructions

The Profit and Loss account is not produced immediately as you must first specify which accounts are to be included in the printout.

Activity

Select SALES and then enter the following:

Category Heading	Low	High
SALES	1000	1000

Then press ESC. This has designated which accounts will be used to calculate sales – the use of the other categories will be considered later.

Now select PURCHASES and enter the following:

Category Heading	Low	High
PURCHASES	2000	2000

Then press ESC, select OVERHEADS (1) and enter the following:

```
Overheads (1)                    Bookkeeper              Date : 170987

████████████████████████████████████████████████████████████████████

                        Category Heading        Low      High

                    WAGES                       4000     4000
                    RENT                        4100     4100
                    RATES                       4200     4200
                    LIGHT & HEAT                4300     4300
                    INSURANCE                   4400     4400
                    MOTOR EXPENSES              4500     4500
                    UNUSED CATEGORY
                    UNUSED CATEGORY
                    UNUSED CATEGORY
                    UNUSED CATEGORY
                    UNUSED CATEGORY
                    UNUSED CATEGORY
                    UNUSED CATEGORY
                    UNUSED CATEGORY
```

Key words   Monthly accounts 26,40,41

Task 28   **Printing out the profit and loss account**

Objective

To print out the Profit and Loss account.

Instructions

You have now configured the Profit and Loss account. In order to get a printout you must first return to the MONTHLY MENU, then select ACCOUNTS PRINTOUT.

```
DUDLEY TRADING PLC              Management Reports - Profit & Loss Account.          Date : 170987
                                                                                    Page :    1

                                       This Month                      Year to Date

        Sales
        -----
        SALES                   1874.75                         1874.75
                                          1874.75                              1874.75
        Purchases
        ---------
        PURCHASES                745.00                          745.00
                                           745.00                               745.00
                                        ------------                          ------------
                                Gross Profit   1129.75          Gross Profit   1129.75

        Overheads
        ---------
        RENT                     100.00                          100.00
        INSURANCE                300.00                          300.00
        MOTOR EXPENSES           118.70                          118.70
                                           518.70                               518.70
                                        ------------                          ------------
                                Nett Profit     611.05          Nett Profit     611.05
                                        ============                          ============
```

Key words

Monthly menu
Profit and loss accounts 26,31,40,41,43

Final check

This is the end of Section B, the next section will examine the sales and purchase ledgers and you will be using new data. You can therefore delete the existing files on your data disk if required.

Section C: Nominal Ledger

Task 29

Re loading the system

The first two sections have demonstrated how SAGE is used to enter simple transactions using the BANK and CASH accounts. They have assumed that the trader using the package had only just started in business. Computerised accounts packages are, however, more likely to be used by firms that have been trading for some time, therefore these firms will have some manual accounting records which they will want to transfer to the computerised system.

This section will show how traders with existing records can set up the SAGE package to include the balances on existing accounts and will also demonstrate more of the MANAGEMENT REPORTS.

It will use fresh data and you should therefore remove the data from the previous sections from your disk. If necessary you can re-format the disk.

Objective

To enter existing accounting records onto the SAGE program.

Instructions

Load the SAGE program and enter the date as 30/09/87, then insert your data disk into the free drive.

As was shown in the last section it is impossible to enter transactions until the required accounts have been 'created'. This means that you will have to set up the control accounts and the nominal accounts again.

Activity

When SAGE has loaded, select the UTILITIES ROUTINES menu and from this menu select INITIALISATION. This option is used to set up the control accounts (i.e. BANK and CASH). You will also be asked to specify the number of accounts required in each ledger. Enter the details as shown:

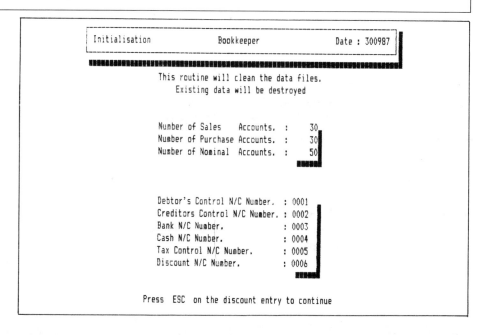

```
 Initialisation              Bookkeeper              Date : 300987

███████████████████████████████████████████████████████████████████
                    This routine will clean the data files.
                       Existing data will be destroyed


                Number of Sales    Accounts. :      30
                Number of Purchase Accounts. :      30
                Number of Nominal  Accounts. :      50
                                                 █████


                Debtor's Control N/C Number. : 0001
                Creditors Control N/C Number. : 0002
                Bank N/C Number.             : 0003
                Cash N/C Number.             : 0004
                Tax Control N/C Number.      : 0005
                Discount N/C Number.         : 0006
                                                 █████

                Press  ESC  on the discount entry to continue
```

Task 30   **Setting up the system**

Objective   To create the accounts required.

Instructions   When you have created the control accounts, follow the screen instructions and press ESC to continue. The program will ask whether you have existing data — the trader does have existing data in his manual records but the program is asking whether you have existing data *on disk*, the answer to this is NO.

Activity   The next step is to set up the nominal accounts needed. To do this return to the MAIN MENU and then select NOMINAL LEDGER POSTINGS. The first item on this menu is NOMINAL ACCOUNTS and this is the option required to set up the accounts. When you are setting up the accounts you will be asked if they are NEW ACCOUNTS. In the trader's opinion they will not be new accounts because he has been trading for years using a *manual* system, but the program is enquiring whether there is already an account created for each item *on disk*, so again the answer will be that all accounts are NEW.

You can now proceed to set-up the Nominal Accounts as follows:

Ref.	Account Name	Ref.	Account Name	Ref.	Account Name
0001	Debtor's Control	0002	Creditors Control	0003	Bank
0004	Cash	0005	Tax Control	0006	Discount
1000	SALES:micro-computers	1001	SALES:printers	1002	SALES:hard disks
2000	PURCHASES:micro-computers	2001	PURCHASES:printers	2002	PURCHASES:hard disks
2003	OPENING STOCK	2004	CLOSING STOCK	3000	COMMISSION
3001	CARRIAGE IN	4000	OFFICE SALARIES	4001	DELIVERY STAFF WAGES
4002	MANAGERS SALARIES	5000	RENT	5001	LIGHT & HEAT
5002	TELEPHONE	5003	STATIONERY	5004	INSURANCE
5005	ADVERTISING	6000	MOTOR REPAIRS	6001	MOTOR EXPENSES
6002	MOTOR INSURANCE	6003	MOTOR TAX	7000	CAPITAL
8000	MOTOR VEHICLES	8001	FIXTURES & FITTINGS	9000	SUSPENSE

Task 31

Objective

Instructions

Entering opening balances

To enter details of amounts already in existence in manual records (opening balances).

You may have noticed that this trader has three accounts for both sales and purchases; this is to enable him to see how well each product performs so that he can produce a more detailed Profit and Loss account.

We can assume that although the trader has been in business for some time he has just ended his financial year and is now about to start a new year. This means that all the accounts for expense items have been cleared via the Profit and Loss account and therefore the only accounts with a balance are for assets, capital and liabilities.

The balances at 1 September 1987 are as follows: motor vehicles £5,000, fixtures and fittings £3,300, opening stock £3,500, bank £2,000, cash £350, debtors £1,750, creditors £1,250 and capital £14,650.

Activity

The JOURNAL is used to enter the initial balances and the comments entered for each entry will be 'opening balance'. Enter the opening balances yourself; remember that errors can be corrected by using the cursor keys and that F2 will copy the details from the previous line. If you cannot enter the opening balances on your own then first select NOMINAL LEDGER POSTINGS and then choose JOURNAL ENTRIES. The reference should be O/BAL and taxe code T9. Enter the rest of the details as shown:

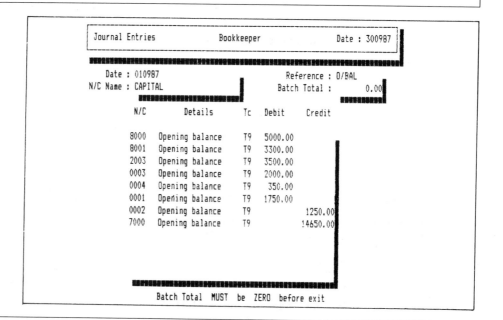

```
Journal Entries            Bookkeeper            Date : 300987

      Date : 010987                      Reference : O/BAL
      N/C Name : CAPITAL                 Batch Total :      0.00

           N/C        Details      Tc   Debit     Credit

           8000    Opening balance  T9  5000.00
           8001    Opening balance  T9  3300.00
           2003    Opening balance  T9  3500.00
           0003    Opening balance  T9  2000.00
           0004    Opening balance  T9   350.00
           0001    Opening balance  T9  1750.00
           0002    Opening balance  T9            1250.00
           7000    Opening balance  T9           14650.00

                   Batch Total  MUST  be  ZERO  before exit
```

Key words
Profit and loss acount 26,28,40,41,43
Journal 12,24
Nominal ledger postings 4,30,37,42
Journal entries 12,13,19,20
Tax code 3
Opening balance 9,54,67

Task 32

Using the function keys

Objective

To use the function keys to speed up data entry.

Instructions

As the date has been set at 30 September 1987 you can enter the details for the whole month. First you will need to enter the bank receipts.

Activity

Select the BANK RECEIPTS option from the menu and then enter the details shown below. Remember that the functions **F1**, **F2** and **F3** can be used to make data entry simpler. If you cannot remember what each function key does then refer back to Task 12.

```
Bank Receipts               Bookkeeper              Date : 300987

███████████████████████████████████████████████████████████████
                                         Tax Rate :      15.000
N/C Name : SALES:printers                Batch Total :  25539.44
         ████████████████████████████                 ██████████

    N/C    Date   Cheque      Details       Nett Amnt Tc Tax Amnt

    1000  020987  234567  F.Kelly             500.00  T1    75.00
    1001  040987  419021  N.Watts             289.75  T1    43.46
    1000  060987  983021  ABC Ltd            2090.50  T1   313.58
    1000  100987  342190  FGH Plc            5090.99  T1   763.65
    1001  100987  342190  FGH Plc            1500.00  T1   225.00
    1002  100987  342190  FGH Plc             750.00  T1   112.50
    1002  130987  109883  J.Hokler            999.99  T1   150.00
    1000  150987  459201  Midshires Council  3500.00  T1   525.00
    1001  150987  459201  Midshires Council  1200.00  T1   180.00
    1000  230987  102901  Walsall Industries 4900.99  T1   735.15
    1000  270987  230987  G.Good              785.99  T1   117.90
    1001  270987  230987  G.Good              599.99  T1    90.00
    █████████████████████████████████████████████████████████
                                            22208.20       3331.24
                                            ████████       ████████
```

Key words

Bank receipts 6,7,8,9,11,16
Function keys 12,55

Task 33

Entering bank payments

Objective

To enter large quantities of transactions.

Activity

When you have completed these transactions you can enter the bank payments. Select the BANK PAYMENTS option and enter the details shown:

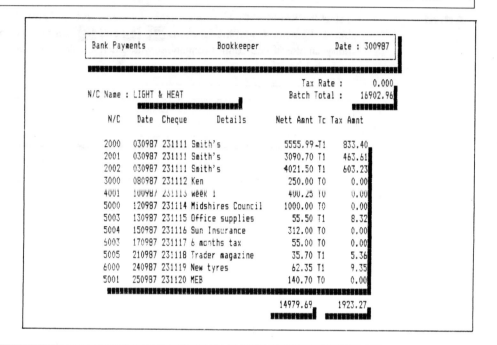

```
Bank Payments              Bookkeeper              Date : 300987

                                           Tax Rate :      0.000
N/C Name : LIGHT & HEAT                    Batch Total :  16902.96

    N/C   Date   Cheque      Details      Nett Amnt Tc Tax Amnt

   2000  030987 231111 Smith's             5555.99 T1  833.40
   2001  030987 231111 Smith's             3090.70 T1  463.61
   2002  030987 231111 Smith's             4021.50 T1  603.23
   3000  080987 231112 Ken                  250.00 T0    0.00
   4001  100987 231113 Week 1               400.25 T0    0.00
   5000  120987 231114 Midshires Council   1000.00 T0    0.00
   5003  130987 231115 Office supplies        55.50 T1    8.32
   5004  150987 231116 Sun Insurance         312.00 T0    0.00
   6003  170987 231117 6 months tax           55.00 T0    0.00
   5005  210987 231118 Trader magazine        35.70 T1    5.36
   6000  240987 231119 New tyres              62.35 T1    9.35
   5001  250987 231120 MEB                   140.70 T0    0.00

                                           14979.69     1923.27
```

Key words

Bank payments 10,11

Task 34

Posting batches

Objective

To post (save) transaction details in batches.

Instructions

The trader has paid out more money than this but you cannot enter any more on the existing screen. The SAGE package will only POST transactions in batches of 12 at a time.

Activity

When you have entered the details from Task 33, POST the transactions and then enter the remaining bank payments on the new screen as follows:

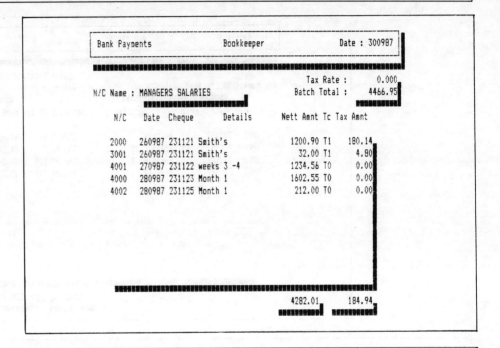

```
Bank Payments              Bookkeeper              Date : 300987

                                            Tax Rate :      0.000
 N/C Name : MANAGERS SALARIES               Batch Total :  4466.95

     N/C    Date  Cheque     Details      Nett Amnt Tc Tax Amnt

     2000  260987 231121 Smith's           1200.90 T1    180.14
     3001  260987 231121 Smith's             32.00 T1      4.80
     4001  270987 231122 weeks 3 -4        1234.56 T0      0.00
     4000  280987 231123 Month 1           1602.55 T0      0.00
     4002  280987 231125 Month 1            212.00 T0      0.00




                                           4282.01       184.94
```

Key words

Post 8,9,11,14,17,20,21,60,74

Task 35   **Entering cash receipts**

Objective   To enter transactions relating to cash receipts.

Instructions   You have now entered the full details of bank receipts and payments for the month of September. The next stage is to enter the cash receipts and payments. As the firm is selling computer hardware, most of the transactions are on credit or paid for by cheque; consequently, there are only a few cash transactions.

Activity   Select the option for CASH RECEIPTS first and enter the following:

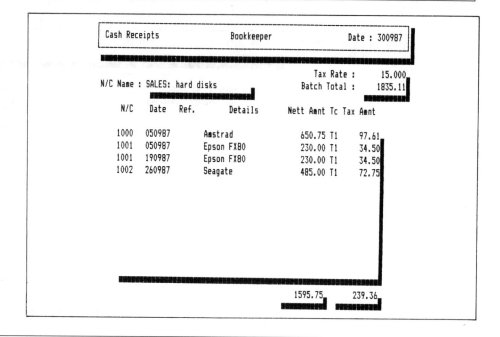

```
Cash Receipts              Bookkeeper              Date : 300987
■■■■■■■■■■■■■■■■■■■■■■■■■■■■■■■■■■■■■■■■■■■■■■■■■■■■■■■■■■■■■■■
                                              Tax Rate :    15.000
         N/C Name : SALES: hard disks         Batch Total :  1835.11
                   ■■■■■■■■■■■■■■■■■■■■                ■■■■■■■■■■
           N/C    Date   Ref.      Details    Nett Amnt Tc Tax Amnt

          1000   050987         Amstrad         650.75 T1   97.61
          1001   050987         Epson FX80      230.00 T1   34.50
          1001   190987         Epson FX80      230.00 T1   34.50
          1002   260987         Seagate         485.00 T1   72.75




          ■■■■■■■■■■■■■■■■■■■■■■■■■■■■■■■■■■■■■■■■■■■■■■■■■
                                             1595.75     239.36
                                             ■■■■■■■■■    ■■■■■■■■■
```

Keywords   Cash receipts 8,14

Task 36   **Entering cash payments**

Objective   To enter transactions relating to cash payments.

Activity   The only payments in cash are for motor expenses and some of the wages. Select the CASH PAYMENTS option and enter the following:

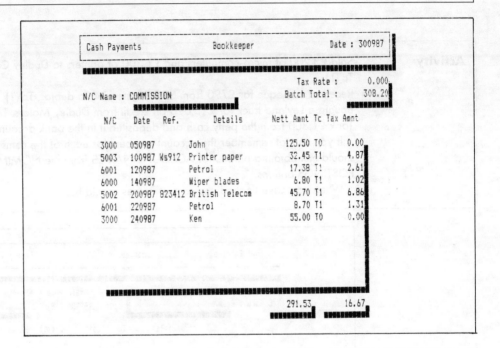

```
Cash Payments              Bookkeeper           Date : 300987

                                            Tax Rate :    0.000
N/C Name : COMMISSION                       Batch Total :  308.20

   N/C   Date   Ref.      Details       Nett Amnt Tc Tax Amnt

   3000  050987            John            125.50 T0     0.00
   5003  100987 Ws912  Printer paper        32.45 T1     4.87
   6001  120987            Petrol           17.38 T1     2.61
   6000  140987            Wiper blades      6.80 T1     1.02
   5002  200987 823412 British Telecom      45.70 T1     6.86
   6001  220987            Petrol            8.70 T1     1.31
   3000  240987            Ken              55.00 T0     0.00




                                          291.53        16.67
```

Key words   **Cash payments 15,16**

Task 37   **Entering credit sales**

Objective

To enter transactions involving credit sales where the sales ledger is not in use.

Instructions

There have been a few sales on credit and the trader has also bought a motor vehicle on credit. These will be entered via the journal so you need to select JOURNAL ENTRIES again. The reference for all entries will be misc. The transactions to be entered in the journal are:

Activity

Sold £3,200 of micro-computers and £1,300 of printers to Dudley Council on credit. Tc (1)

Received a cheque for £790 from SDF Engineering, a debtor. Tc (1)

Bought a Leyland truck for £15,090 on credit from Dudley Motors. Tc (1)

Took £1,300 from the petty cash and deposited it in the bank account. Tc (0)

If you cannot remember the account numbers for each of the items then you should first obtain a printout of ACCOUNT NAMES from the NOMIMAL LEDGER POSTINGS options.

When you have finished, the correct entries should be:

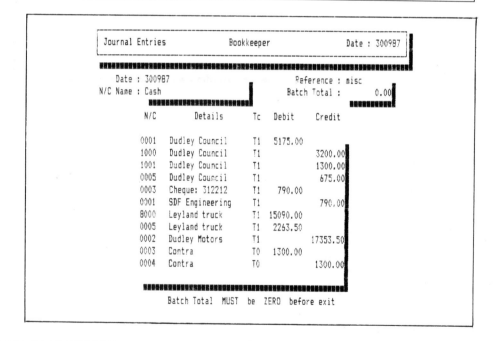

```
 Journal Entries              Bookkeeper            Date : 300987

      Date : 300987                    Reference : misc
   N/C Name : Cash                     Batch Total :        0.00

        N/C       Details      Tc    Debit     Credit

        0001   Dudley Council   T1   5175.00
        1000   Dudley Council   T1              3200.00
        1001   Dudley Council   T1              1300.00
        0005   Dudley Council   T1               675.00
        0003   Cheque: 312212   T1    790.00
        0001   SDF Engineering  T1               790.00
        8000   Leyland truck    T1  15090.00
        0005   Leyland truck    T1   2263.50
        0002   Dudley Motors    T1             17353.50
        0003   Contra           T0   1300.00
        0004   Contra           T0              1300.00

            Batch Total MUST be ZERO before exit
```

Key words

Journal entries 12,13,14,19,20,42

Account names 21

Nominal ledger postings 4,30,31,42

Task 38   The quick ratio

Objective   To obtain the nominal ledger report on the quick ratio.

Instructions   You have now entered all of the transactions for this month's trading. The next step is to examine some of the reports available using SAGE.

Return to the MAIN MENU and then select NOMINAL LEDGER REPORTS.

Some of these items were examined in Section B, but you have not yet used the QUICK RATIO report. Select this now. The quick ratio is a statement of the firm's liquidity position. 'Liquidity' is best described as a firm's ability to pay its debts; therefore the quick ratio compares current assets with current liabilities.

Activity   In order to use the quick ratio option you must first inform the program which accounts should be included in the calculation. To do this choose the EDIT option.

Enter the N/C numbers for all of the current assets and current liabilities. If you have already obtained a printout of account names you should be able to identify these accounts yourself. Try to enter the details on your own before checking that they are correct. If you make any mistakes these can easily be rectified, either by using the cursor keys or by re-selecting the EDIT option.

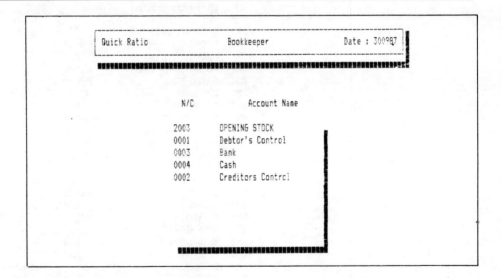

```
Quick Ratio              Bookkeeper              Date : 300987
```

N/C	Account Name
2003	OPENING STOCK
0001	Debtor's Control
0003	Bank
0004	Cash
0002	Creditors Control

Keywords   **Nominal ledger reports 17,21,39**
Quick ratio 22,39
Edit 8,9,39

Task 39   The Trial Balance

Objective

To obtain the nominal ledger report on the Trial Balance.

Instructions

If you have entered the account numbers correctly, exit the EDIT mode by pressing `ESC`.

Activity

Re-select QUICK RATIO and choose the VIEW option. The following will appear either on screen or as a printout. This shows that the firm has a 'Working Capital' of £132.06, which leaves it in a difficult position.

    If you return to the NOMINAL LEDGER REPORTS menu you can now select the TRIAL BALANCE option. Obtain a printout of the Trial Balance as you will need a 'hard copy' later.

Ref.	Accounts Name	Debit	Credit
0001	Debtor's Control	6135.00	
0002	Creditors Control		18603.50
0003	Bank	8259.53	
0004	Cash	576.91	
0005	Tax Control	142.78	
1000	SALES:micro-computers		20719.22
1001	SALES:printers		5349.74
1002	SALES:hard disks		2234.99
2000	PURCHASES:micro-computers	6756.89	
2001	PURCHASES:printers	3090.70	
2002	PURCHASES:hard disks	4021.50	
2003	OPENING STOCK	3500.00	
3000	COMMISSION	430.50	
3001	CARRIAGE IN	32.00	
4000	OFFICE SALARIES	1602.55	
4001	DELIVERY STAFF WAGES	1634.81	
4002	MANAGERS SALARIES	212.00	
5000	RENT	1000.00	
5001	LIGHT & HEAT	140.70	
5002	TELEPHONE	45.70	
5003	STATIONERY	87.95	
5004	INSURANCE	312.00	
5005	ADVERTISING	35.70	
6000	MOTOR REPAIRS	69.15	
6001	MOTOR EXPENSES	26.08	
6003	MOTOR TAX	55.00	
7000	CAPITAL		14650.00
8000	MOTOR VEHICLES	20090.00	
8001	FIXTURES & FITTINGS	3300.00	
		61557.45	61557.45

Key words

Edit 8,9,38
Quick ratio 22,38
View
Nominal ledger reports 17,21,38
Trial Balance 21

Task 40

Configuring the Profit and Loss account

Objective

To design the layout of a simple Profit and Loss account.

Instructions

You have created three accounts for both sales and purchases. This will enable you to obtain a better analysis of results. Initially though, you can obtain a standard Profit and Loss account.

Activity

Select MONTHLY ACCOUNTS from the MANAGEMENT REPORTS menu. Before producing a Profit and Loss account it must be 'configured' to include the required accounts. Select PROFIT AND LOSS and proceed to configure the Profit and Loss account as follows: first select the SALES option which should be entered as:

CATEGORY HEADING	LOW	HIGH
SALES	1000	1002

Press **ENTER** to move the next line and then press **ESC** to exit the SALES category. The other categories can be configured as follows:

CATEGORY	CATEGORY HEADING	LOW	HIGH
PURCHASES	PURCHASES	2000	2004
DIRECT EXPENSES	DIRECT EXPENSES	3000	3001
OVERHEADS (1)	WAGES & SALARIES	4000	4002
OVERHEADS (2)	OFFICE EXPENSES	5000	5005
OVERHEADS (3)	MOTOR EXPENSES	6000	6003

Key words

Profit and Loss account 26,28,31,41,43
Configure 2,3
Monthly accounts 26,27,41
Management reports 24,43,63,64

Task 41 **Examining the management report**

Objective To obtain the management report of the Profit and Loss account.

Instruction Perhaps you can now see why the different N/C numbers were chosen. While this configuration will not show the sales and purchases of the different products, it will categorise the various expenses into the various groups. This printout will show the totals paid for all expenses within each category (i.e. total wages, total office expenses, total motor expenses).

Activity You can now return to the MONTHLY ACCOUNTS menu and choose ACCOUNTS PRINTOUT from that menu. This should produce the following Profit and Loss account:

```
DUDLEY TRADING PLC              Management Reports - Profit & Loss Account.          Date : 300987
                                                                                     Page :    1

                               This Month                        Year to Date

         Sales
         -----
         SALES               28303.95                          28303.95
                                            28303.95                            28303.95
         Purchases
         ---------
         PURCHASES           17369.09                          17369.09
                                            17369.09                            17369.09
         Direct Expenses
         ---------------
         DIRECT EXPENSES       462.50                            462.50
                                              462.50                              462.50
                                         --------------                     --------------
                             Gross Profit  10472.36            Gross Profit   10472.36

         Overheads
         ---------
         WAGES & SALARIES     3449.36                           3449.36
         OFFICE EXPENSES      1622.05                           1622.05
         MOTOR EXPENSES        150.23                            150.23
                                             5221.64                             5221.64
                                         --------------                     --------------
                             Nett Profit    5250.72            Nett Profit     5250.72
                                         ==============                     ==============
```

Key words **Monthly accounts 26,27,40**
Accounts printout
Profit and loss account 26,28,31,40,43

Task 42   **Handling closing stock**

Objective

To deal with closing stock at the end of a period.

Instructions

This Profit and Loss account is a summary of the totals for each category chosen but you can re-configure it to show the full details for each individual account.

Before you re-configure the Profit and Loss account there is one adjustment that should be made. If you refer back to Task 32 you can see that you have created an account for closing stock with an N/C number of 2004. There is no entry in this account yet.

The total for closing stock does not form part of the double-entry accounting system and is usually ascertained by counting all stock at the end of the year. Our trader calculates that his closing stock is worth £3,200. However, this amount cannot be included in the Profit and Loss account if it is not entered in the closing stock account and it can not be entered in the closing stock account unless there is a 'double entry' somewhere else. The solution is to make a journal entry and create a temporary account called a SUSPENSE account.

Activity

Return to the NOMINAL LEDGER POSTINGS menu and make the following entry under JOURNAL ENTRIES:

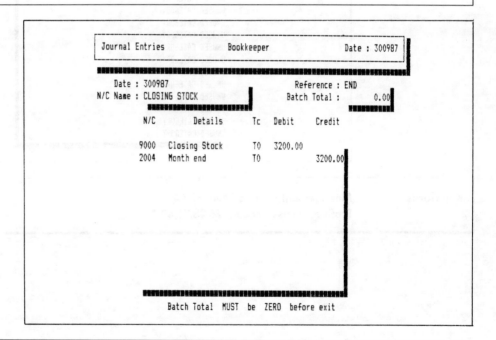

```
Journal Entries          Bookkeeper              Date : 300987
████████████████████████████████████████████████████████████████████

    Date : 300987                    Reference : END
N/C Name : CLOSING STOCK             Batch Total :        0.00
         ████████████████████████        █████████████

         N/C       Details     Tc   Debit     Credit

         9000   Closing Stock   T0   3200.00
         2004   Month end       T0             3200.00




         ██████████████████████████████████████████████████
                 Batch Total  MUST  be  ZERO  before exit
```

Key words

Journal entries 12,13,14,19,20,37
Suspense account
Nominal ledger postings 4,30,31,37

Task 43   **Reconfiguring the Profit and Loss account**

Objective   To design the layout of a more detailed Profit and Loss account.

Instructions   You can now return to the MANAGEMENT REPORTS menu and re-configure the Profit and Loss account by selecting the PROFIT AND LOSS option once again.

Activity   Choose SALES as before but this time change the headings and entries as follows:

```
Sales                    Bookkeeper              Date : 300987
█████████████████████████████████████████████████████████████

                  Category Heading        Low       High

                  Microcomputers          1000      1000
                  Printers                1001      1001
                  Hard Disks              1002      1002
                  UNUSED CATEGORY
                  UNUSED CATEGORY
                  UNUSED CATEGORY
                  UNUSED CATEGORY
                  UNUSED CATEGORY
                  UNUSED CATEGORY
                  UNUSED CATEGORY
                  UNUSED CATEGORY
                  UNUSED CATEGORY
                  UNUSED CATEGORY
                  UNUSED CATEGORY
                  UNUSED CATEGORY
                  █████████████████████████████████████████
```

Key words   **Management reports 24,40,63,64**
                     Profit and Loss account 26,28,31,40,41

Task 44

Configuring the purchase accounts

Objective

To include the various purchase accounts in a Profit and Loss account.

Activity

Your next step is to select the PURCHASES category. Re-enter these as shown:

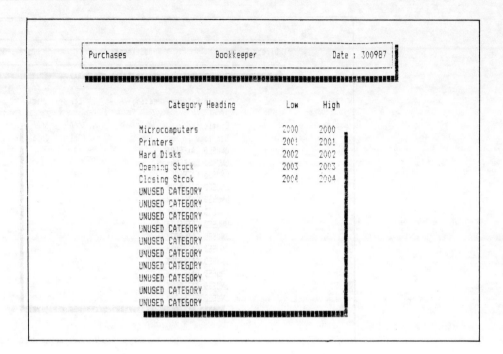

Purchases	Bookkeeper		Date : 300987

Category Heading	Low	High
Microcomputers	2000	2000
Printers	2001	2001
Hard Disks	2002	2002
Opening Stock	2003	2003
Closing Stock	2004	2004
UNUSED CATEGORY		
UNUSED CATEGORY		
UNUSED CATEGORY		
UNUSED CATEGORY		
UNUSED CATEGORY		
UNUSED CATEGORY		
UNUSED CATEGORY		
UNUSED CATEGORY		
UNUSED CATEGORY		
UNUSED CATEGORY		

Task 45

Configuring the direct expenses

Objective

To include direct expenses in a Profit and Loss account.

Activity

You will also need to adjust the entries for direct expenses. Enter these as follows:

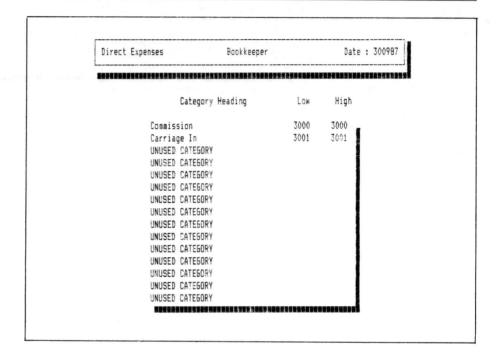

```
┌──────────────────────────────────────────────────────────────┐
│ Direct Expenses          Bookkeeper           Date : 300987    │
└──────────────────────────────────────────────────────────────┘
████████████████████████████████████████████████████████████████

                    Category Heading       Low    High

                  Commission               3000   3000
                  Carriage In              3001   3001
                  UNUSED CATEGORY
                  UNUSED CATEGORY
                  UNUSED CATEGORY
                  UNUSED CATEGORY
                  UNUSED CATEGORY
                  UNUSED CATEGORY
                  UNUSED CATEGORY
                  UNUSED CATEGORY
                  UNUSED CATEGORY
                  UNUSED CATEGORY
                  UNUSED CATEGORY
                  UNUSED CATEGORY
                  UNUSED CATEGORY
                 ████████████████████████████████████████
```

Task 46

Configuring overheads

Objective   To include overheads in the Profit and Loss account.

Activity   The final step is to adjust the overheads so that full details of each account total are shown. Select overheads (1) and enter the revised details as shown:

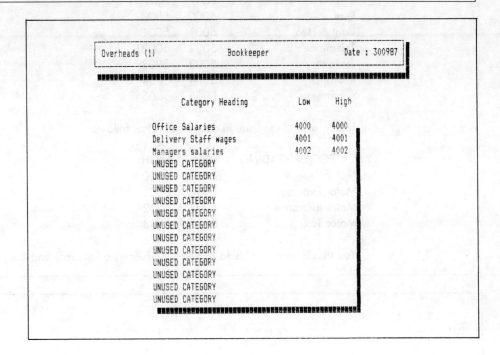

```
Overheads (1)              Bookkeeper              Date : 300987


                    Category Heading        Low     High

                Office Salaries             4000    4000
                Delivery Staff wages        4001    4001
                Managers salaries           4002    4002
                UNUSED CATEGORY
                UNUSED CATEGORY
                UNUSED CATEGORY
                UNUSED CATEGORY
                UNUSED CATEGORY
                UNUSED CATEGORY
                UNUSED CATEGORY
                UNUSED CATEGORY
                UNUSED CATEGORY
                UNUSED CATEGORY
                UNUSED CATEGORY
```

Task 47   Administration overheads

Objective   To specify overheads by category/type in a Profit and Loss account.

Activity   You can now adjust the items in overheads (2) as follows:

CATEGORY HEADING	LOW	HIGH
Rent	5000	5000
Light & Heat	5001	5001
Telephone	5002	5002
Stationery	5003	5003
Insurance	5004	5004
Advertising	5005	5005

Finally, amend the items in overheads (3) as follows:

CATEGORY HEADING	LOW	HIGH
Motor Repairs	6000	6000
Motor Expenses	6001	6001
Motor Insurance	6002	6002
Motor Tax	6003	6003

You should now be able to produce the following full profit and loss account.

```
JDLEY TRADING PLC              Management Reports - Profit & Loss Account.            Date : 300987
                                                                                     Page :    1

                                   This Month                      Year to Date

        Sales
        -----
        Microcomputers            20719.22                         20719.22
        Printers                   5349.74                          5349.74
        Hard Disks                 2234.99                          2234.99
                                                28303.95                          28303.95

        Purchases
        ---------
        Microcomputers             6756.89                          6756.89
        Printers                   3090.70                          3090.70
        Hard Disks                 4021.50                          4021.50
        Opening Stock              3500.00                          3500.00
        Closing Stcok       (      3200.00)                  (      3200.00)
                                                14169.09                          14169.09

        Direct Expenses
        ---------------
        Commission                  430.50                           430.50
        Carriage In                  32.00                            32.00
                                                  462.50                            462.50
                                                -------------                     -------------
                            Gross Profit        13672.36      Gross Profit        13672.36
```

```
Overheads
---------
Office Salaries            1602.55                          1602.55
Delivery Staff wages       1634.81                          1634.81
Managers salaries           212.00                           212.00
Rent                       1000.00                          1000.00
Light & Heat                140.70                           140.70
Telephone                    45.70                            45.70
Stationery                   87.95                            87.95
Insurance                   312.00                           312.00
Advertising                  35.70                            35.70
Motor Repairs                69.15                            69.15
Motor Expenses               26.08                            26.08
Motor Tax                    55.00                            55.00
                                        5221.64                          5221.64
                                        --------                         --------
                        Nett Profit     8450.72          Nett Profit     8450.72
                                        ============                     ============
```

Task 48

Objective

Instructions

The Balance Sheet

To obtain a detailed Profit and Loss account report and prepare a balance sheet.

The SAGE package does not produce a Balance Sheet as it is primarily designed as a simple book-keeping program. The Profit and Loss accounts produced are also very simple versions and in practice are only included so that the trader can have a rough idea of how his business is doing each month. The Trial Balance and other printouts would still be submitted to the trader's accountant at the end of the year and the proper Trading and Profit and Loss account and balance sheet would be drawn up by the accountant.

Activity

To conclude this section, use the Trial Balance to draft the balance sheet as it would appear at 30 September 1987.

Key words   **Balance Sheet**

Section D: Sales and Purchase Ledgers ▬▬▬

Task 49

The 'division of ledgers'

Objective

To understand the concept of the 'division of ledgers'.

This section introduces the other two functions of the SAGE package, namely the sales and purchase ledgers. Before you attempt this section you should make sure that you understand why there are different ledgers.

In the previous section it has been assumed that the records are being kept for a small firm, probably a sole trader, therefore most of his transactions will be for cash (or cheque). Firms of this size do not require very complicated record systems, nor do they need many accounts.

Instructions

A larger organisation will be more likely to operate most of its transactions on a 'credit' system. Goods are bought and sold on 'credit' and paid for in the following month. This means that the firm must keep some accounts to record the amounts owed to and by each individual debtor and creditor.

The simplest way of dealing with the credit transactions is to keep the 'credit' accounts in different sections of the system, therefore, all accounts for debtors are stored in the sales ledger and all accounts for creditors are kept in the purchases ledger. All transactions for debtors or creditors will require a 'double-entry' in the other ledger (the nominal ledger); for example, if someone buys goods on credit from the firm then there will be entries as follows:

Debit: Debtors account

Credit: Sales account

To save having to continually switch between ledgers, the program will make the other entry for you and pass the double-entry through the control accounts. The procedure is as follows:

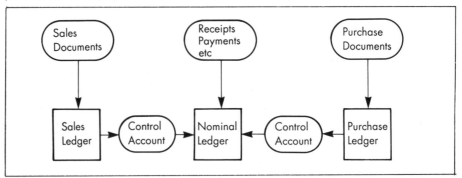

Using the different ledgers

Objective   To delete records relating to previous sections.

Instructions   Another advantage of splitting accounts between the different ledgers is that it enables the firm to produce a more varied range of reports, as you will see later in this section.

Before beginning this section you are recommended to re-format your disk. Failing this, clear all files of suffix DTA.

The suffix DTA refers to DATA and files with this suffix which contain the account details of all the transactions that you have entered. If you delete these files you will have no records left. Under normal circumstances this would be a disaster but as this is only a training manual the old records are no longer needed.

Details of old transactions can also be deleted by re-initiating the system. When you select the UTILITIES option for this you will be given a warning by the program that all existing data will be destroyed. Therefore if you are unable to get into the operating system you can rely on the system initialisation option to delete all files of type DTA for you.

Load SAGE and enter the date as 30/09/87. The password is LETMEIN.

Activity   Before entering any data you will have to initialise the system for your requirements. Select the UTILITIES option and then initialise the system to set the number of accounts required as shown:

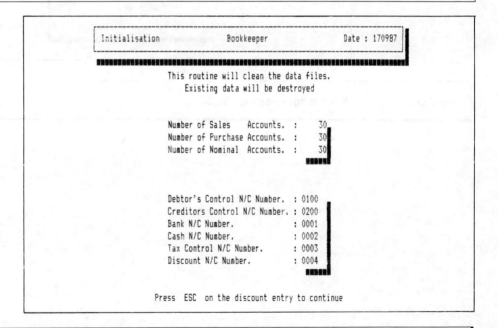

```
Initialisation            Bookkeeper            Date : 170987

This routine will clean the data files.
Existing data will be destroyed


              Number of Sales    Accounts. :      30
              Number of Purchase Accounts. :      30
              Number of Nominal  Accounts. :      30



              Debtor's Control N/C Number.  : 0100
              Creditors Control N/C Number. : 0200
              Bank N/C Number.              : 0001
              Cash N/C Number.              : 0002
              Tax Control N/C Number.       : 0003
              Discount N/C Number.          : 0004

         Press  ESC  on the discount entry to continue
```

Key words   Initialise 3,29
Utilities
Suffix DTA

Task 51   **Creating debtors' accounts**

Objective   To create an account for a debtor (customer) in the sales ledger.

Activity	The next step is to set up the accounts for the debtors. Select the SALES LEDGER POSTINGS option and you should obtain the following menu.
	This shows the options available for recording data relating to debtors. As you can see, the only options are to examine/set up accounts for debtors' (accounts), record sales (invoices), record goods returned (credit notes) and record payments received (receipts).

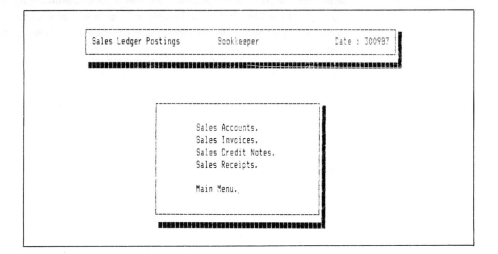

Key words	**Sales ledger postings 56,66**

Task 52

Entering account details

Objective

To enter debtors' account details.

Instructions

Transactions can only be entered when an account is in existence for that particular debtor so the SALES ACCOUNTS function has to be used to set up accounts for each debtor before any transactions can be entered. This function is also used to set up existing balances for debtors when the firm is converting from a manual to a computerised system.

The SALES ACCOUNTS function can be selected and the first account details entered.

The first account is for a debtor called RS Smith Ltd. The account reference could be a number as in the nominal ledger but the program does not allow you to use text as account references in both the sales and purchase ledgers. Therefore you can enter the account reference as SMITH, as this is easier to remember than a number.

Activity

The account name is RS SMITH LTD and you can enter this in the appropriate space. The next prompt will ask you if this is a new account; this is actually asking you if you already have this account on another disk. You have not so the answer is YES. The address can be entered over 4 lines and is SMITH HOUSE, OLDBURY, WEST MIDLANDS, OD3 5RT. If you have entered these details correctly the screen should show the following:

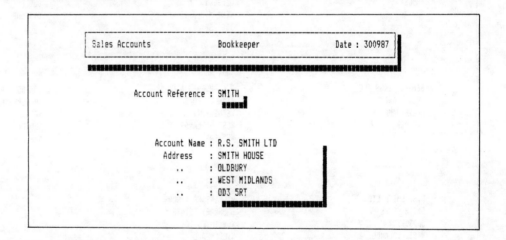

```
 Sales Accounts              Bookkeeper            Date : 300987

 ███████████████████████████████████████████████████████████████

           Account Reference : SMITH
                              ▄▄▄▄▄█


           Account Name : R.S. SMITH LTD
           Address      : SMITH HOUSE
                 ..      : OLDBURY
                 ..      : WEST MIDLANDS
                 ..      : OD3 5RT
                        ████████████████████████
```

Key words

Sales accounts 56
Account details

Task 53   **Creating additional accounts**

Objective   To creating additional accounts for debtors.

Activity   When you have entered the account details for Smith you can create accounts for the other debtors. The account references to use are:

ABCLTD
DCRLTD
DOUGIE
GEMFIT
HUGHES
ROMBOL
WILKIN

The full names and addresses are shown below. When you have entered the details correctly, save the data and proceed to the next item by pressing ESC .

ABC LIMITED	DCR LIMITED	DOUGIES EMPORIUM
WEST STREET	NEW ESTATE	HIGH STREET
DUDLEY	OLDBURY	DUDLEY
DY4 3WS	WEST MIDLANDS	DY4 5HF
	OD4 2SB	
GEM FITTINGS PLC	P.C. HUGHES & CO	ROM BOLT AND NUTS
BROAD LANE	STANLEY ROAD	GREGORY INDUSTRIAL ESTATE
WOLVERHAMPTON	WEDNESBURY	NETHERTON
WV3 8SB	WEST MIDLANDS	DUDLEY
	WE5 6AS	DY6 2GH
R.S. SMITH LTD	WILKINSONS & SONS	
SMITH HOUSE	BOUNDARY ESTATE	
OLDBURY	NEW INVENTION	
WEST MIDLANDS	WILLENHALL	
OD3 5RT	WH8 1JK	

Key words   Debtors' accounts

Task 54

Debtors' opening balances

Objective

To enter opening balances for debtors.

Instructions

You can assume that the firm has already been trading for a month and therefore these accounts already have some entries which need to be transferred to the computer system. To enter opening balances the SALES INVOICES are required.

The sales invoices option works in a very similar way to the cash and bank payments/receipts options in the nominal ledger, in that twelve invoices can be posted at a time.

Activity

The first opening balance to post can be that for RS Smith Ltd. Enter the account name as SMITH and the full name should appear at the top of the screen. As the opening balance will be the amount owed at 1st September you can enter the date as 010987. The invoice reference for opening balances should always be O/BAL. The next item is the N/C – this is a request for the account needed for the double-entry in the nominal ledger. Normally this would be the sales account (or one of them) but for opening balances it is the debtors' control account, the number of which is 0100. Enter the details as opening balance and the nett amount as £1000. The tax code for opening balances is T9 (not subject to tax).

You should have the following screen:

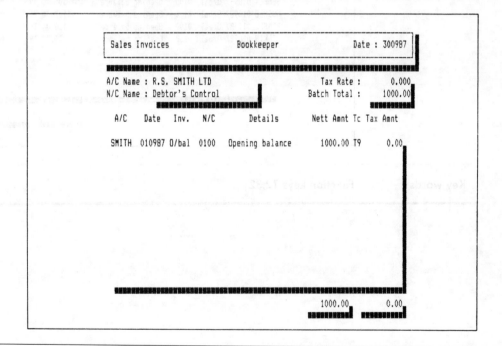

Key words

Opening balance 9,31,67
Sales invoices 60,63

Task 55

Copying data

To use the function key F2 to copy data.

Activity

The other accounts created also have opening balances and you can enter these as shown in the following display. Remember that the function key F2 will copy the entry from the preceding line and make data entry much simpler. Any errors can easily be adjusted by moving the cursor with the aid of the cursor keys.

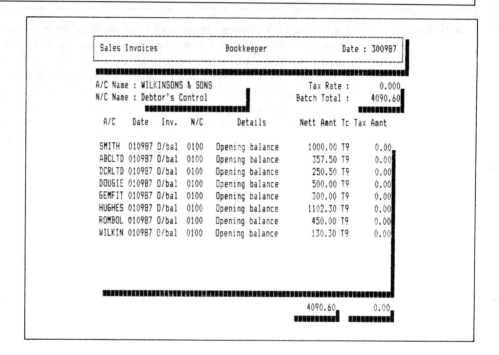

```
Sales Invoices              Bookkeeper              Date : 300987

A/C Name : WILKINSONS & SONS                  Tax Rate :      0.000
N/C Name : Debtor's Control                   Batch Total :  4090.60

  A/C    Date   Inv.   N/C      Details      Nett Amnt Tc Tax Amnt

 SMITH 010987 O/bal  0100   Opening balance   1000.00 T9    0.00
 ABCLTD 010987 O/bal 0100   Opening balance    357.50 T9    0.00
 DCRLTD 010987 O/bal 0100   Opening balance    250.50 T9    0.00
 DOUGIE 010987 O/bal 0100   Opening balance    500.00 T9    0.00
 GEMFIT 010987 O/bal 0100   Opening balance    300.00 T9    0.00
 HUGHES 010987 O/bal 0100   Opening balance   1102.30 T9    0.00
 ROMBOL 010987 O/bal 0100   Opening balance    450.00 T9    0.00
 WILKIN 010987 O/bal 0100   Opening balance    130.30 T9    0.00




                                               4090.60      0.00
```

Key words   Function keys 12,32

Task 56   Creating sales and purchase accounts

Objective

To create sales and purchases accounts in the nominal ledger.

Instructions

The system is now almost ready to start accepting new transactions. Any new sales will require a double entry that will consist of one entry in the debtors' account and one entry in the sales account. However, no sales account has yet been created, so before proceeding you will have to go to the nominal ledger and set up accounts for the sales accounts.

Exit the SALES LEDGER POSTINGS option and select NOMINAL ACCOUNTS from the nominal ledger postings menu.

Activity

The firm is now involved in selling office equipment and requires sales accounts for each of the different types of product sold. While you are creating these accounts, set up the purchase accounts and expense accounts at the same time. Create the accounts as shown:

Ref.	Account Name	Ref.	Account Name	Ref.	Account Name
0100	Debtor's Control	0200	Creditors Control	0300	Bank
0400	Cash	0500	Tax Control	0600	Discount
1000	Sales: desks	1001	Sales: Filing Cabinets	1002	Sales: chairs
1003	Sales: Miscellaneous	2000	Purchases: Desks	2001	Purchases:Filing Cabinets
2002	Purchases: Chairs	2003	Purchases: Miscellaneous	3000	Rent & Rates
3001	Office Expenses	4000	Motor expenses	4001	Motor repairs
5000	Selling expenses				

Key words

Sales ledger postings 51,66
Nominal accounts 5,30
Sales accounts 52

Task 57

Creating creditors' accounts

Objective

To enter details and create accounts for creditors' (suppliers).

Instructions

Set up the opening balances on the creditors' accounts in the purchase ledger; the creditors' accounts will need to be created first. The procedure is identical to the sales ledger except that it is accessed through the PURCHASE LEDGER POSTINGS option.

Activity

Create the accounts for the following creditors; all accounts are new accounts:

DUDLEY
HERON
OFFICE
OFFSUP

The full names and addresses are as follows:

```
DUDLEY COUNCIL          E & R HERON LTD          OFFICE FITTINGS LTD
RATES OFFICE            NEW ESTATE               NEW STREET
NEW ROAD                HALESOWEN                BIRMINGHAM
DUDLEY                  WEST MIDLANDS            B13 5RT
DY1 6WE                 HS6 2WM



OFFICE SUPPLIES PLC
GRANGE ROAD
RUGBY
RY7 1DF
```

Key words   **Purchase ledger postings 74**

Task 58 — Entering opening balances

Objective

To enter details of amounts already owed to suppliers (opening balances).

Once you have entered these details you can select the PURCHASE INVOICES option and enter the opening balances as follows (*Note* the F2 key will make data entry easier):

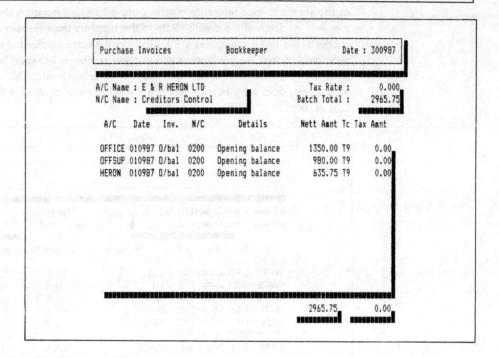

```
Purchase Invoices          Bookkeeper              Date : 300987

A/C Name : E & R HERON LTD                    Tax Rate :      0.000
N/C Name : Creditors Control                  Batch Total :  2965.75

A/C    Date   Inv.   N/C    Details        Nett Amnt Tc Tax Amnt

OFFICE 010987 O/bal  0200   Opening balance  1350.00 T9    0.00
OFFSUP 010987 O/bal  0200   Opening balance   980.00 T9    0.00
HERON  010987 O/bal  0200   Opening balance   635.75 T9    0.00




                                             2965.75        0.00
```

Key words Purchase invoices 59

Task 59

Entering invoice details

Objective
To enter details of purchases on credit.

Instructions
When you have entered these details press **ESC** and then POST them but do not exit the PURCHASE INVOICES option.

Activity
While you are in the purchase invoices option, enter the invoice details for the month as shown: the invoice reference numbers are the invoice numbers shown on the suppliers invoice and the details relate to the suppliers stock number for the different products. The first three entries are taken from the same invoice but are entered separately so that Dudley Trading can analyse purchases between the different products (i.e. N/C 2000: desks, N/C 2001: filing cabinets, etc). This makes more work during data entry but will produce a much greater analysis in the Profit and Loss account.

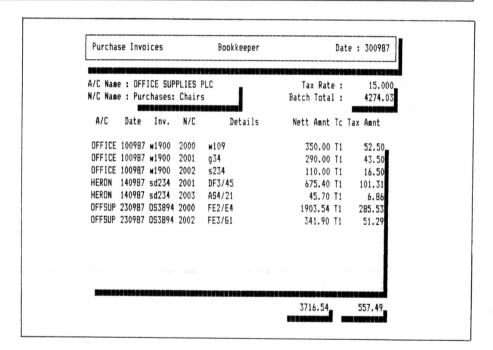

```
Purchase Invoices          Bookkeeper          Date : 300987


A/C Name : OFFICE SUPPLIES PLC              Tax Rate :      15.000
N/C Name : Purchases: Chairs               Batch Total :   4274.03

   A/C    Date   Inv.   N/C     Details      Nett Amnt Tc Tax Amnt

   OFFICE 100987 w1900  2000    w109            350.00 T1    52.50
   OFFICE 100987 w1900  2001    g34             290.00 T1    43.50
   OFFICE 100987 w1900  2002    s234            110.00 T1    16.50
   HERON  140987 sd234  2001    DF3/45          675.40 T1   101.31
   HERON  140987 sd234  2003    AS4/21           45.70 T1     6.86
   OFFSUP 230987 OS3894 2000    FE2/E4         1903.54 T1   285.53
   OFFSUP 230987 OS3894 2002    FE3/G1          341.90 T1    51.29




                                             3716.54      557.49
```

Key words   **Purchase invoices 58**

Task 60   **Entering sales invoices**

Objective   To enter details of sales on credit.

Instructions   Once you have correctly entered these details you can POST them and then return to the sales ledger and select SALES INVOICES.

Activity   The details for sales invoices are entered in the same way but the invoice reference numbers in this case are all sequentially numbered as they have been sent out by the firm. The details differ from the purchase invoice as the details now record Dudley Trading's stock numbers.

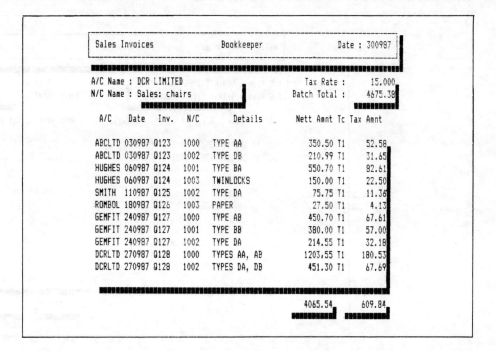

```
Sales Invoices              Bookkeeper              Date : 300987
████████████████████████████████████████████████████████████████

A/C Name : DCR LIMITED                        Tax Rate :      15.000
N/C Name : Sales: chairs                      Batch Total :  4675.38
                      ████████████████

    A/C   Date   Inv.   N/C      Details      Nett Amnt Tc Tax Amnt

    ABCLTD 030987 Q123  1000  TYPE AA           350.50 T1   52.58
    ABCLTD 030987 Q123  1002  TYPE DB           210.99 T1   31.65
    HUGHES 060987 Q124  1001  TYPE BA           550.70 T1   82.61
    HUGHES 060987 Q124  1003  TWINLOCKS         150.00 T1   22.50
    SMITH  110987 Q125  1002  TYPE DA            75.75 T1   11.36
    ROMBOL 180987 Q126  1003  PAPER              27.50 T1    4.13
    GEMFIT 240987 Q127  1000  TYPE AB           450.70 T1   67.61
    GEMFIT 240987 Q127  1001  TYPE BB           380.00 T1   57.00
    GEMFIT 240987 Q127  1002  TYPE DA           214.55 T1   32.18
    DCRLTD 270987 Q128  1000  TYPES AA, AB     1203.55 T1  180.53
    DCRLTD 270987 Q128  1002  TYPES DA, DB      451.30 T1   67.69
████████████████████████████████████████████████████

                                              4065.54      609.84
```

Key words   **Post** 8,9,11,14,17,20,21,34,74
                            Sales invoices 54,63

Task 61

Entering sales returns

Objective

To enter details of sales returns.

Instructions

Unfortunately, some of the goods sold to ABC Ltd on 3 September 1987 and some of the goods sold to Gem Fittings Ltd on 24 September 1987 have been returned as damaged or unsuitable. These firms have sent Dudley Trading a credit note to inform them that they will not be paying for them and that we should make a credit entry in their account.

Activity

Enter these details using the SALES CREDIT NOTES option as they are shown.

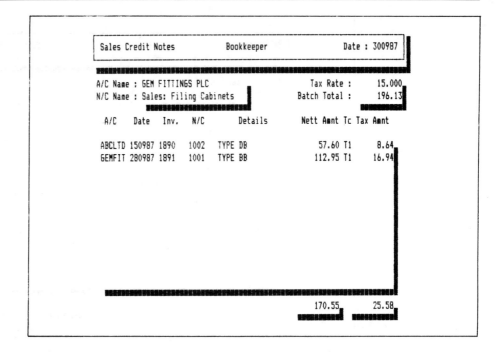

```
Sales Credit Notes          Bookkeeper              Date : 300987

A/C Name : GEM FITTINGS PLC                  Tax Rate :      15.000
N/C Name : Sales: Filing Cabinets            Batch Total :    196.13

   A/C    Date   Inv.   N/C      Details      Nett Amnt Tc Tax Amnt

ABCLTD 150987 1890    1002    TYPE DB           57.60 T1     8.64
GEMFIT 280987 1891    1001    TYPE BB          112.95 T1    16.94




                                               170.55       25.58
```

Key words

Sales credit notes 63

Task 62

Entering purchase returns

Objective

To enter details of purchase returns.

Instructions

Dudley Trading is a retailer and the items that have been returned were bought in from a supplier, so if they are damaged the obvious thing to do is to return them. They are returned to the supplier with a credit note informing them that Dudley Trading will not be paying for the goods and that they should make a credit entry in their account. This document is often referred to as a debit note because a debit entry will be made in the suppliers' account. The system appears to be reversed because the supplier is Dudley Trading's creditor, whereas the supplier considers them as one of his debtors.

Activity

Select the PURCHASE CREDIT NOTES option and enter the details as follows:

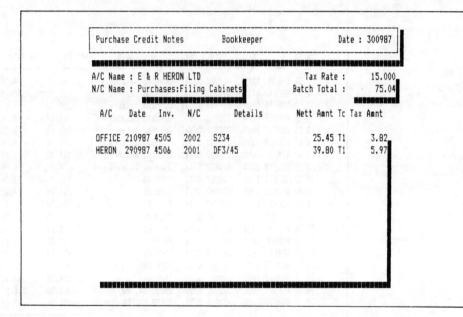

Key words   **Purchase credit notes**

Task 63 **Examining sales invoices**

Objective

To examine the sales ledger report on the sales daybook and sales returns.

Instructions

You can now examine some of the reports available from the sales and purchase ledgers. Select the MANAGEMENT REPORTS option.

Activity

The first item is for DAYBOOKS and if you select this option you can see that a daybook can be produced for each of the entry types in the sales ledger. Select SALES INVOICES and press **ENTER** in response to each of the questions. You should get the following printout or screen display:

```
DUDLEY TRADING PLC                          Day Books - Sales Invoices.


No. Tp  A/C    N/C   Date    Ref.      Details       Nett Am'nt Tax Am'nt Gross Amount Tc
---- --  ------ ----- ------  ------   ------------------  ----------  ---------- ----------- --
   1 SI SMITH  0100   010987 O/bal  Opening balance     1000.00       0.00     1000.00  T9
   2 SI ABCLTD 0100   010987 O/bal  Opening balance      357.50       0.00      357.50  T9
   3 SI DCRLTD 0100   010987 O/bal  Opening balance      250.50       0.00      250.50  T9
   4 SI DOUGIE 0100   010987 O/bal  Opening balance      500.00       0.00      500.00  T9
   5 SI GEMFIT 0100   010987 O/bal  Opening balance      300.00       0.00      300.00  T9
   6 SI HUGHES 0100   010987 O/bal  Opening balance     1102.30       0.00     1102.30  T9
   7 SI ROMBOL 0100   010987 O/bal  Opening balance      450.00       0.00      450.00  T9
   8 SI WILKIN 0100   010987 O/bal  Opening balance      130.30       0.00      130.30  T9
  19 SI ABCLTD 1000   030987 0123   TYPE AA              350.50      52.58      403.08  T1
  20 SI ABCLTD 1002   030987 0123   TYPE DB              210.99      31.65      242.64  T1
  21 SI HUGHES 1001   060987 0124   TYPE BA              550.70      82.61      633.31  T1
  22 SI HUGHES 1003   060987 0124   TWINLOCKS            150.00      22.50      172.50  T1
  23 SI SMITH  1002   110987 0125   TYPE DA               75.75      11.36       87.11  T1
  24 SI ROMBOL 1003   180987 0126   PAPER                 27.50       4.13       31.63  T1
  25 SI GEMFIT 1000   240987 0127   TYPE AB              450.70      67.61      518.31  T1
  26 SI GEMFIT 1001   240987 0127   TYPE BB              380.00      57.00      437.00  T1
  27 SI GEMFIT 1002   240987 0127   TYPE DA              214.55      32.18      246.73  T1
  28 SI DCRLTD 1000   270987 0128   TYPES AA, AB        1203.55     180.53     1384.08  T1
  29 SI DCRLTD 1002   270987 0128   TYPES DA, DB         451.30      67.69      518.99  T1
                                                     ---------- ---------- -----------
                                                       8156.14     609.84     8765.98
```

Key words

Management reports 24,40,43,64
Daybooks 25,81
Sales invoices 54,60
Sales credit notes 61

This is simply a summary of all the entries made under the SALES INVOICES option. The option for SALES CREDIT NOTES will produce the following printout or screen display:

```
        DUDLEY TRADING PLC              Day Books - Sales Credit Notes.



        No. Tp  A/C    N/C    Date   Ref.      Details      Nett Am'nt Tax Am'nt Gross Amount  Tc
        ---- -- ------ ----   ------ -----     --------     ---------- --------- -----------   --
         30 SC ABCLTD 1002  150987 1890     TYPE DB            57.60     8.64      66.24      T1
         31 SC GEMFIT 1001  280987 1891     TYPE BB           112.95    16.94     129.89      T1
                                                             ---------- --------- -----------
                                                                170.55    25.58     196.13
```

Task 64

The audit trail

Objective

To examine the management report on the audit trail when all ledgers are being used.

Instructions

These printouts are useful when a firm is making very large numbers of entries as they are often very difficult to check. However, as we have only a small number of entries, the audit trail will be a more useful printout.

Activity

This is obtained from the MANAGEMENT REPORTS menu; see if you can obtain a printout.

```
No. Type A/C    N/C   Details              Date   Inv.   Nett Amount Tax Amount  TC  Paid  Date  Cheque Amount Paid N-AC N-NC
---- ---- ------ ----  ------------------   ------ -----  ----------- ----------  --- ----  ----- ------ -----------  ---- ----
   1 SI   SMITH  0100  Opening balance      010987 O/bal    1000.00       0.00    T9   N                       0.00   23    2
   2 SI   ABCLTD 0100  Opening balance      010987 O/bal     357.50       0.00    T9   N                       0.00   19    3
   3 SI   DCRLTD 0100  Opening balance      010987 O/bal     250.50       0.00    T9   N                       0.00   28    4
   4 SI   DOUGIE 0100  Opening balance      010987 O/bal     500.00       0.00    T9   N                       0.00    0    5
   5 SI   GEMFIT 0100  Opening balance      010987 O/bal     300.00       0.00    T9   N                       0.00   25    6
   6 SI   HUGHES 0100  Opening balance      010987 O/bal    1102.30       0.00    T9   N                       0.00   21    7
   7 SI   ROMBOL 0100  Opening balance      010987 O/bal     450.00       0.00    T9   N                       0.00   24    8
   8 SI   WILKIN 0100  Opening balance      010987 O/bal     130.30       0.00    T9   N                       0.00    0    0
   9 PI   OFFICE 0200  Opening balance      010987 O/bal    1350.00       0.00    T9   N                       0.00   12   10
  10 PI   OFFSUP 0200  Opening balance      010987 O/bal     980.00       0.00    T9   N                       0.00   17   11
  11 PI   HERON  0200  Opening balance      010987 O/bal     635.75       0.00    T9   N                       0.00   15    0
  12 PI   OFFICE 2000  W109                 100987 w1900     350.00      52.50    T1   N                       0.00   13   17
  13 PI   OFFICE 2001  G34                  100987 w1900     290.00      43.50    T1   N                       0.00   14   15
  14 PI   OFFICE 2002  S234                 100987 w1900     110.00      16.50    T1   N                       0.00   32   18
  15 PI   HERON  2001  DF3/45               140987 SD234     675.40     101.31    T1   N                       0.00   16   33
  16 PI   HERON  2003  AS4/21               140987 SD234      45.70       6.86    T1   N                       0.00   33    0
  17 PI   OFFSUP 2000  FE2/E4               230987 OS3894    1903.54     285.53   T1   N                       0.00   18    0
  18 PI   OFFSUP 2002  FE3/61               230987 OS3894     341.90      51.29   T1   N                       0.00    0   32
  19 SI   ABCLTD 1000  TYPE AA              030987 G123       350.50      52.58   T1   N                       0.00   20   25
  20 SI   ABCLTD 1002  TYPE DB              030987 G123       210.99      31.65   T1   N                       0.00   30   23
  21 SI   HUGHES 1001  TYPE BA              060987 G124       550.70      82.61   T1   N                       0.00   22   26
  22 SI   HUGHES 1003  TWINLOCKS            060987 G124       150.00      22.50   T1   N                       0.00    0   24
  23 SI   SMITH  1002  TYPE DA              110987 G125        75.75      11.36   T1   N                       0.00    0   27
  24 SI   ROMBOL 1003  PAPER                180987 G126        27.50       4.13   T1   N                       0.00    0    0
  25 SI   GEMFIT 1000  TYPE AB              240987 G127       450.70      67.61   T1   N                       0.00   26   28
  26 SI   GEMFIT 1001  TYPE BB              240987 G127       380.00      57.00   T1   N                       0.00   27   31
  27 SI   GEMFIT 1002  TYPE DA              240987 G127       214.55      32.18   T1   N                       0.00   31   29
  28 SI   DCRLTD 1000  TYPES AA, AB         270987 G128      1203.55     180.53   T1   N                       0.00   29    0
  29 SI   DCRLTD 1002  TYPES DA, DB         270987 G128       451.30      67.69   T1   N                       0.00    0   30
  30 SC   ABCLTD 1002  TYPE DB              150987 1890        57.60       8.64   T1   N                       0.00    0    0
  31 SC   GEMFIT 1001  TYPE BB              280987 1891       112.95      16.94   T1   N                       0.00    0    0
  32 PC   OFFICE 2002  S234                 210987 4505        25.45       3.82   T1   N                       0.00    0    0
  33 PC   HERON  2001  DF3/45               290987 4506        39.80       5.97   T1   N                       0.00    0    0
```

Final check

If you compare this with the other printouts you can see that each transaction is given its own number (i.e. 1–34) and can therefore be checked off in all the printouts. The audit trail also shows the type of transaction (e.g. SI = Sales Invoice) and the fact that no account has yet been paid by or paid to Dudley Trading. This will be covered in the next section.

The N–AC column refers to the next entry made in the same account, the next entry of SMITH is number 23 on 11/09/87. The N–NC column refers to the next transaction which also had a double-entry in the same nominal ledger account.

Section E: Sales and purchase ledgers ▄▄▄

Task 65

Examining account balances

Objective

To examine the account balances of debtors.

Instructions

The last section showed how the sales and purchase ledgers are used to create accounts for customers and suppliers where the transaction is on a credit basis. It is obviously important to keep records of how much each customer/supplier has outstanding as the account will need to be cleared at some point.

This section assumes that a month has passed since the last section and that some of the customers have sent in payments for the amounts owing. Load SAGE as previously instructed and set the date to 31/10/87.

Before proceeding to make the entries for this month it is worthwhile reminding ourselves what accounts are on disk. Therefore, when the SAGE menu appears select the option for SALES LEDGER REPORTS.

Activity

Select the option for ACCOUNT BALANCES and when the next prompts appear press ENTER for both lower account reference and upper account reference (this will then include all accounts in the report). You can then opt for a screen display or printout.

```
DUDLEY TRADING PLC                      Sales Ledger Reports - Account Balances.


A/C        Account Name       Balance   Current    30 days    60 Days    90 Days    Older
-----      ------------       -------   -------    -------    -------    -------    -----
ABCLTD  ABC LIMITED            936.98      0.00     579.48     357.50       0.00      0.00
DCRLTD  DCR LIMITED           2153.57      0.00    1903.07     250.50       0.00      0.00
DOUGIE  DOUGIES EMPORIUM       500.00      0.00       0.00     500.00       0.00      0.00
GEMFIT  GEM FITTINGS PLC      1372.15      0.00    1072.15     300.00       0.00      0.00
HUGHES  P.C. HUGHES & CO      1908.11      0.00     805.81    1102.30       0.00      0.00
ROMBOL  ROM BOLT AND NUTS      481.63      0.00      31.63     450.00       0.00      0.00
SMITH   R.S. SMITH LTD        1087.11      0.00      87.11    1000.00       0.00      0.00
WILKIN  WILKINSONS & SONS      130.30      0.00       0.00     130.30       0.00      0.00
                              -------   -------    -------    -------    -------    -----
                 Totals :     8569.85      0.00    4479.25    4090.60       0.00      0.00
```

Key words

Sales ledger reports
Account balances

67

Task 66

Entering debtors' payments

Objective

To enter details of payments received from debtors.

Instructions

This report shows the amount outstanding on each of the accounts in the sales ledger; the 'history' of each account shows how long the balances have been outstanding. SAGE has recognised that you are now in a different month and has updated the account 'histories' automatically. This means that it is never necessary to 'close' accounts at the end of each month.

As we are in the next month some of the customers have started to send in payments for the amounts that they owe. Return to the main menu and then select SALES LEDGER POSTINGS. Most of the options on this menu were covered in the last section, with the exception of SALES RECEIPTS. Select this option now.

Activity

The first account to be updated will be for ABC Limited, the A/C reference for this account is ABCLTD. Type this in when the program has loaded SALES RECEIPTS. The program will check that this account reference exists and should then print ABC LIMITED in the section for A/C Name.

Enter the date of payment as 22/10/87 (*Note* this will have to be typed as 221087) and the cheque number as 435555. The amount paid was £357.50 which can be entered as the cheque amount. The screen will then show details of all the transactions currently held on the account for ABCLTD.

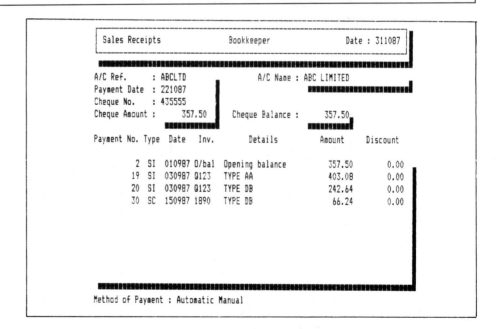

```
 Sales Receipts              Bookkeeper            Date : 311087

 ▬▬▬▬▬▬▬▬▬▬▬▬▬▬▬▬▬▬▬▬▬▬▬▬▬▬▬▬▬▬▬▬▬▬▬▬▬▬▬▬▬▬▬▬▬▬▬▬▬▬▬▬▬▬▬▬
 A/C Ref.      : ABCLTD            A/C Name : ABC LIMITED
 Payment Date  : 221087                     ▬▬▬▬▬▬▬▬▬▬▬▬▬▬▬▬▬▬▬▬▬▬
 Cheque No.    : 435555
 Cheque Amount :      357.50       Cheque Balance :    357.50
                     ▬▬▬▬▬▬▬▬                      ▬▬▬▬▬▬▬▬

 Payment No. Type  Date   Inv.      Details        Amount   Discount

          2   SI  010987 O/bal  Opening balance     357.50     0.00
         19   SI  030987 0123   TYPE AA             403.08     0.00
         20   SI  030987 0123   TYPE DB             242.64     0.00
         30   SC  150987 1890   TYPE DB              66.24     0.00




 ▬▬▬▬▬▬▬▬▬▬▬▬▬▬▬▬▬▬▬▬▬▬▬▬▬▬▬▬▬▬▬▬▬▬▬▬▬▬▬▬▬▬▬▬▬▬▬▬▬▬▬▬▬▬▬▬
 Method of Payment : Automatic Manual
```

Key words

Account history 22,23,76,77,78,79
Sales ledger postings 51,56
Sales receipts

Task 67 — Matching payments

Objective To match payments with amounts owing using the automatic option.

Instructions The prompt is now at the bottom of the screen and is waiting for you to decide how you want to deal with this payment. In SAGE, payments need to be allocated (i.e. matched) to a corresponding transaction. This matching can be done *automatically* by SAGE, in which case the payments will always be set off against the oldest transaction, or *manually* where the operator can select which transaction should be paid off.

If you examine the details of transactions it should be apparent that the payment relates to the transaction no 2 from 1/10/87 for the opening balance. Therefore the payment can be allocated using the automatic option.

Activity Press ENTER to select AUTOMATIC. The screen display should alter to show that:
(i) the cheque balance is nil (i.e. the full amount has been set off).
(ii) the amount owing for transaction no 2 has been paid in full.

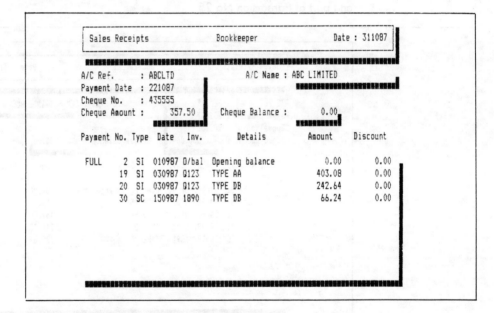

```
Sales Receipts              Bookkeeper           Date : 311087
▇▇▇▇▇▇▇▇▇▇▇▇▇▇▇▇▇▇▇▇▇▇▇▇▇▇▇▇▇▇▇▇▇▇▇▇▇▇▇▇▇▇▇▇▇▇▇▇▇▇▇▇▇▇
A/C Ref.     : ABCLTD          A/C Name : ABC LIMITED
Payment Date : 221087                    ▇▇▇▇▇▇▇▇▇▇▇▇▇▇▇▇▇▇▇▇
Cheque No.   : 435555
Cheque Amount :      357.50    Cheque Balance :     0.00
                    ▇▇▇▇▇▇▇▇▇                  ▇▇▇▇▇▇▇▇▇

Payment No. Type  Date   Inv.     Details       Amount    Discount

FULL    2  SI  010987 D/bal  Opening balance      0.00      0.00
       19  SI  030987 0123   TYPE AA            403.08      0.00
       20  SI  030987 0123   TYPE DB            242.64      0.00
       30  SC  150987 1890   TYPE DB             66.24      0.00
```

Key words   **Transaction 2,5,8,12,13,15,16,17,18,73,79,81**
Matching 69,72,75
Opening balances 9,31,54

Task 68   Part payments

Objective   To enter details of 'part payments'.

Instructions   If you have done this correctly press `ESC` to accept the allocation and then
press `ENTER` to POST the transaction details. Posting the transaction will ensure that the
account for ABCLTD will be updated and that the money received will be debited to the
bank account in the nominal ledger.

Activity   The next payment received was from Gem Fittings and was a cheque for £500.00
dated 23/10/87, cheque number 908765. The account reference for Gem Fittings is
GEMFIT. Enter these details.

    If you have done this correctly you should be presented with the screen shown
below. If you examine the transactions listed it should be apparent that Gem Fittings
have not sent the payment for any one particular transaction but have sent a
payment on account. This amount covers more than one transaction and therefore
needs to be set off against more than one transaction. It covers the opening balance
and part of transaction No 25.

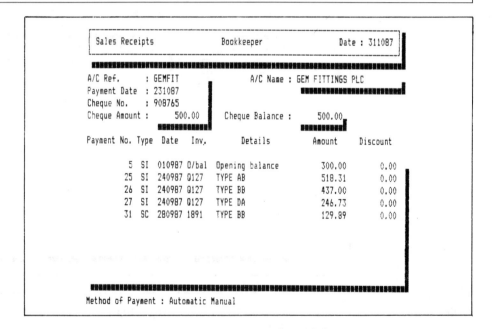

```
┌─────────────────────────────────────────────────────────────────────────┐
│  Sales Receipts              Bookkeeper            Date : 311087          │
│  ████████████████████████████████████████████████████████████████████    │
│  A/C Ref.     : GEMFIT              A/C Name : GEM FITTINGS PLC            │
│  Payment Date : 231087                        █████████████████████████   │
│  Cheque No.   : 908765                                                    │
│  Cheque Amount :      500.00    Cheque Balance :    500.00                │
│                  █████████████                   ███████████              │
│                                                                           │
│  Payment No. Type  Date   Inv.      Details       Amount    Discount      │
│                                                                           │
│          5   SI  010987  O/bal   Opening balance   300.00      0.00       │
│         25   SI  240987  Q127    TYPE AB           518.31      0.00        │
│         26   SI  240987  Q127    TYPE BB           437.00      0.00        │
│         27   SI  240987  Q127    TYPE DA           246.73      0.00        │
│         31   SC  280987  1891    TYPE BB           129.89      0.00        │
│                                                                           │
│  ████████████████████████████████████████████████████████████████████    │
│  Method of Payment : Automatic Manual                                     │
└─────────────────────────────────────────────────────────────────────────┘
```

Key words   Posting transactions 8,9

Task 69   Automatic matching

Objective   To allocate part-payment details by using the automatic option.

Instructions   Even though the payment does not exactly 'match' any particular transaction it can still be allocated using the automatic option.

Activity   Press ENTER to select automatic — the screen should show a new line of options: full, part, discount and cancel.

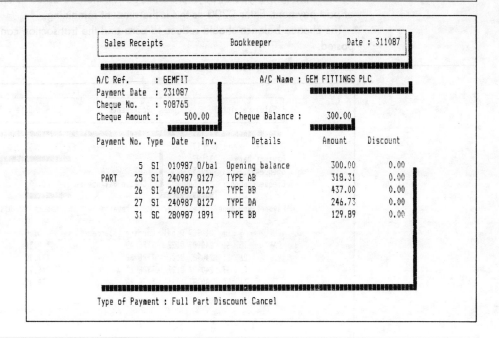

```
Sales Receipts              Bookkeeper              Date : 311087

A/C Ref.      : GEMFIT            A/C Name : GEM FITTINGS PLC
Payment Date  : 231087
Cheque No.    : 908765
Cheque Amount :      500.00     Cheque Balance :     300.00

Payment No. Type Date   Inv.     Details        Amount    Discount

            5  SI  010987 O/bal  Opening balance  300.00     0.00
     PART   25  SI  240987 Q127   TYPE AB          318.31     0.00
            26  SI  240987 Q127   TYPE BB          437.00     0.00
            27  SI  240987 Q127   TYPE DA          246.73     0.00
            31  SC  280987 1891   TYPE BB          129.89     0.00

Type of Payment : Full Part Discount Cancel
```

Key words   Matching 67,72,75

Task 70   Matching payments

Objective

To match payments until the cheque balance becomes zero.

Instructions

The first line (transaction no 5) is then highlighted and FULL appears in the column for payment. Press `ENTER` to accept this as the payment will be used to pay the oldest amount first. The cursor should then move to the next line for transaction No 25. The top of the screen shows that the CHEQUE BALANCE is £200.00.

Activity

Select PART as the type of payment and you will then be asked to enter the amount of part payment. Enter £200 as this is the amount remaining.

The cheque balance should reduce to zero and the transaction can then be posted.

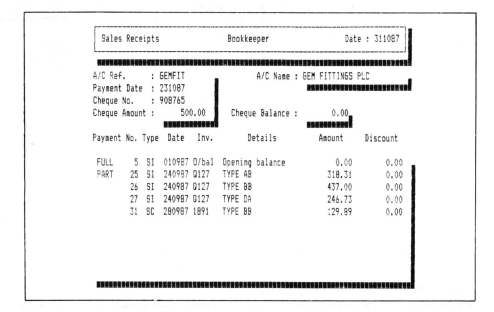

```
 Sales Receipts              Bookkeeper            Date : 311087


 A/C Ref.     : GEMFIT            A/C Name : GEM FITTINGS PLC
 Payment Date : 231087
 Cheque No.   : 908765
 Cheque Amount :      500.00    Cheque Balance :      0.00

 Payment No. Type  Date   Inv.      Details      Amount    Discount

 FULL    5  SI  010987 O/bal  Opening balance      0.00       0.00
 PART   25  SI  240987 0127   TYPE AB            318.31       0.00
        26  SI  240987 0127   TYPE BB            437.00       0.00
        27  SI  240987 0127   TYPE DA            246.73       0.00
        31  SC  280987 1891   TYPE BB            129.89       0.00
```

Key words   Part payment

Task 71

Matching payments

Objective

To enter details of payments which involve discount for prompt payment.

Instructions

The next payment is a cheque numbered 109902 for £110.00 from Wilkinson & Sons, dated 2/10/87. This is A/C ref WILKIN. Call up this account and enter the appropriate details.

This account has only one entry which is the opening balance of £130.30. The amount paid is in full settlement of the account – the difference being discount that Dudley Trading has given to Wilkinsons & Sons for prompt payment of their account.

Activity

Select MANUAL as the method of allocation and when asked to select type of payment choose DISCOUNT.

The next prompt will ask for the amount of discount which will be the balance remaining after the cheque has been paid. Opening balance £130.30 – cheque £110.00 = discount £20.30. Enter £20.30 as the discount:

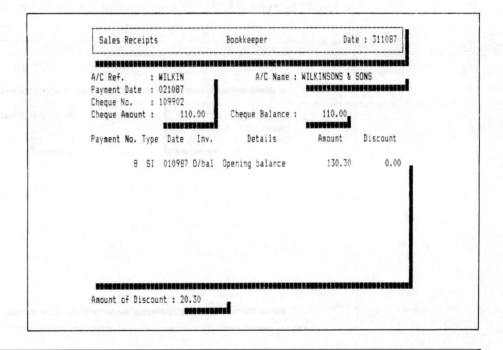

```
Sales Receipts          Bookkeeper          Date : 311087

A/C Ref.     : WILKIN          A/C Name : WILKINSONS & SONS
Payment Date : 021087
Cheque No.   : 109902
Cheque Amount :    110.00    Cheque Balance :    110.00

Payment No. Type Date   Inv.     Details      Amount    Discount

         8  SI  010987 O/bal  Opening balance   130.30      0.00

Amount of Discount : 20.30
```

Key words   Discount 72,79

73

Task 72

Allocating discount

Objective

To allocate discount amounts to a specific transaction.

Instructions

When the opening balance is marked discount, post the entry. The amount entered for discount will automatically be posted into the discount control account in the nominal ledger.

The other type of entry that will be needed is to 'match' credit notes with invoices. Remember that credit notes are used to signify that some goods have been returned as unsuitable; at some point they will need to be matched with the original invoice that recorded the sale of the goods.

Activity

Gem Fittings have received a credit note that can now be matched to the invoice. Call up the details for GEMFIT again.

There is no cheque as no payment has been received. Enter the date as 31/10/87 and the cheque No as 000000.

Select MANUAL as the type of payment, then move the cursor to the transaction of type SC (sales credit note). You can now select FULL as the type of payment.

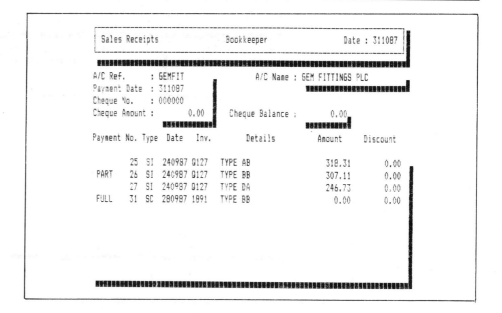

```
| Sales Receipts              Bookkeeper              Date : 311087 |

A/C Ref.    : GEMFIT              A/C Name : GEM FITTINGS PLC
Payment Date : 311087
Cheque No.   : 000000
Cheque Amount :        0.00    Cheque Balance :       0.00

Payment No. Type Date   Inv.      Details        Amount    Discount

         25 SI  240987 0127    TYPE AB          318.31      0.00
PART     26 SI  240987 0127    TYPE BB          307.11      0.00
         27 SI  240987 0127    TYPE DA          246.73      0.00
FULL     31 SC  280987 1891    TYPE BB            0.00      0.00
```

Key words

Discount 71,79
Credit notes 73
Matching 67,69,75

Task 73

Matching credit notes

Objective

To update accounts to show reductions in respect of credit nots.

Instructions

Note that the cheque balance has increased to £129.89. The next step is to identify which invoice this credit note related to. The only other transaction involving TYPE BB' was no 26 on 24/09/87 which was for £437.00 in total so not all of these products were returned. This means that only part of this transaction can be cleared as Gem Fittings still owe the balance.

Activity

Move the cursor to no 26 as the corresponding invoice and press ENTER. Then select FULL (you are not paying the invoice in full but you are allocating the FULL amount of the cheque balance against this transaction). The cheque balance should reduce to zero.

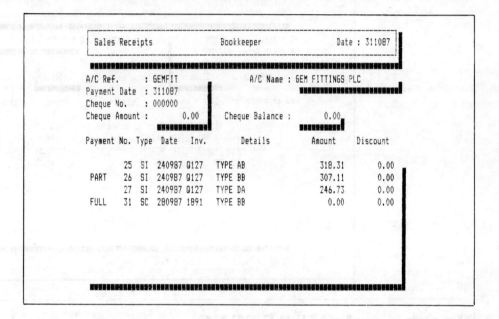

```
Sales Receipts            Bookkeeper           Date : 311087
███████████████████████████████████████████████████████████
A/C Ref.    : GEMFIT          A/C Name : GEM FITTINGS PLC
Payment Date : 311087                  ████████████████████████
Cheque No.  : 000000
Cheque Amount :      0.00    Cheque Balance :      0.00
                  ████████████             ███████████
Payment No. Type Date  Inv.    Details        Amount  Discount

        25  SI  240987 0127  TYPE AB         318.31    0.00
PART    26  SI  240987 0127  TYPE BB         307.11    0.00
        27  SI  240987 0127  TYPE DA         246.73    0.00
FULL    31  SC  280987 1891  TYPE BB           0.00    0.00
```

Key words

Credit notes 72
Transaction 2,5,8,12,13,15,16,17,18,67,79,81

Making payments

Objective   To enter details of payments made to suppliers.

Instructions   If the entry has been done correctly you can then POST this transaction.
Payments for purchases are very similar to receipts from sales so you can now update
the purchases ledger to record payments made to suppliers. Exit the sales ledger and
call up the purchase ledger postings menu.

Activity   Dudley Trading has made a payment to E & R Heron Ltd by cheque number
234109 on 18/10/87 for £1366.69. The A/C ref. for E & R Heron is HERON. Call
up Heron's account and enter the following details:

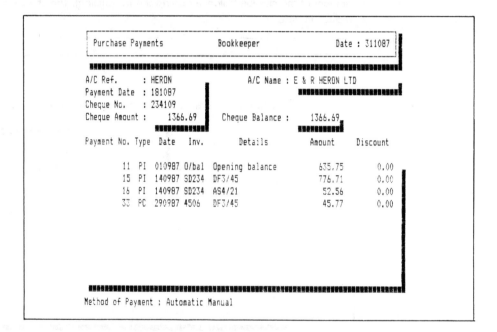

```
 Purchase Payments          Bookkeeper            Date : 311087

████████████████████████████████████████████████████████████████

A/C Ref.    : HERON              A/C Name : E & R HERON LTD
Payment Date : 181087            ██████████████████████████████
Cheque No.  : 234109
Cheque Amount :    1366.69       Cheque Balance :    1366.69
                 ███████████████                ███████████

Payment No. Type  Date   Inv.      Details        Amount   Discount

       11   PI  010987  O/bal   Opening balance     635.75      0.00
       15   PI  140987  SD234   DF3/45              776.71      0.00
       16   PI  140987  SD234   AS4/21               52.56      0.00
       33   PC  290987  4506    DF3/45               45.77      0.00




████████████████████████████████████████████████████████████████

Method of Payment : Automatic Manual
```

Key words   **Post** 8,9,11,14,17,20,21,34,60
Purchases ledger 49,77
Purchases ledger postings 57

Task 75   **Entering payments manually**

Objective

To enter payments using the manual option.

Instructions

The payment of £1366.69 is payment for transaction Nos 11 and 15. The difference relates to those goods that the firm returned and to which the purchase credit note (No 34) relates. This means that the 'purchase payment' will involve matching the payment with amounts outstanding and clearing the credit note.

Activity

Select MANUAL as the method for allocating payments and then select the type of payment as FULL for transaction nos 11 and 15. This should reduce the cheque payment amount to −£45.77. Move the cursor to transaction no 34 and select payment type FULL again. This will reduce both the credit note amount and the cheque balance to zero.

    These details can then be posted.

    It is possible to check in the account for HERON that these transactions have been recorded properly. Exit the purchase ledger postings section and select PURCHASE LEDGER REPORTS.

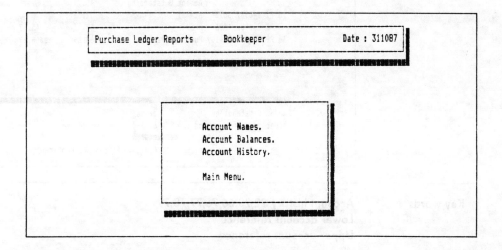

```
Purchase Ledger Reports      Bookkeeper            Date : 311087
```

```
        Account Names.
        Account Balances.
        Account History.

        Main Menu.
```

Key words

Matching 67,69,72
Purchase ledger reports 77

Task 76   **Examining account details**

Objective   To examine the account details of creditors using the purchase ledger reports.

Activity   Select the item for ACCOUNT HISTORY. This could be used to examine all accounts at once, but for the present we need only consider the account for HERON. When asked to provide the LOWER and UPPER ACCOUNT REFERENCE, enter HERON. You are then given the option of having the report produced on the screen or to the printer. Select whichever you prefer.

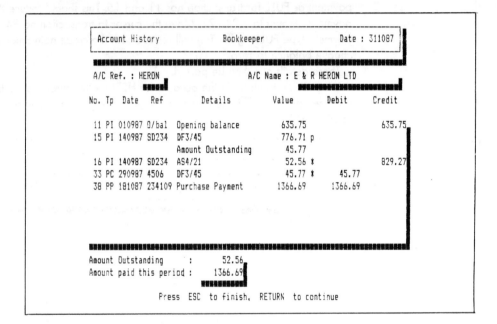

```
Account History          Bookkeeper              Date : 311087

A/C Ref. : HERON                    A/C Name : E & R HERON LTD

No. Tp Date   Ref       Details         Value     Debit     Credit

11 PI 010987 O/bal  Opening balance     635.75              635.75
15 PI 140987 SD234  DF3/45              776.71 p
                    Amount Outstanding   45.77
16 PI 140987 SD234  AS4/21               52.56 ‡            829.27
33 PC 290987 4506   DF3/45               45.77 ‡   45.77
38 PP 181087 234109 Purchase Payment   1366.69   1366.69


Amount Outstanding      :      52.56
Amount paid this period :    1366.69
              Press ESC to finish, RETURN to continue
```

Key words   **Account history 22,23,66,76,77,78,79**
Lower account reference
Upper account reference

Task 77

Interpreting account details

Objective

To interpret the details shown in the account history report.

Instructions

The account history shows details of all transactions. It does not delete those items that have been paid as the information will still be required to enable the user to check how payments have been disposed of.

The account history shows that there is only £52.56 outstanding and that this relates to transaction no 16. The * is used to denote items that are still outstanding. Note also that the account history has entered the various transactions under the columns for debit and credit. This is done automatically by the program and saves the user from having to learn which items are to be debited and which are to be credited.

The reports produced by the SALES LEDGER and the PURCHASES LEDGER are identical except for the fact that one refers to customers and the other to suppliers. To prove this you can exit the PURCHASE LEDGER REPORTS menu and select SALES LEDGER REPORTS. The options available are the same under both menus.

Activity

Examine the ACCOUNT BALANCES report in the sales ledger. The program will ask you to specify the range of accounts that you would like to examine – ask for all accounts. To do this press ENTER in response to both LOWER and UPPER RANGES. Once again, specify whether the printout is to be sent to the screen or to the printer.

```
DUDLEY TRADING PLC                    Sales Ledger Reports - Account Balances.


A/C      Account Name       Balance    Current    30 days    60 Days    90 Days    Older
------   ----------------   --------   --------   --------   --------   --------   --------
ABCLTD   ABC LIMITED         579.48       0.00     579.48       0.00       0.00       0.00
DCRLTD   DCR LIMITED        2153.57       0.00    1903.07     250.50       0.00       0.00
DOUGIE   DOUGIES EMPORIUM    500.00       0.00       0.00     500.00       0.00       0.00
GEMFIT   GEM FITTINGS PLC    872.15       0.00     872.15       0.00       0.00       0.00
HUGHES   P.C. HUGHES & CO   1908.11       0.00     805.81    1102.30       0.00       0.00
ROMBOL   ROM BOLT AND NUTS   481.63       0.00      31.63     450.00       0.00       0.00
SMITH    R.S. SMITH LTD     1087.11       0.00      87.11    1000.00       0.00       0.00
                           ---------   --------   --------   --------   --------   --------
              Totals :      7582.05       0.00    4279.25    3302.80       0.00       0.00
```

Key words

Account history 22,23,66,76,78,79
Sales ledger 49
Purchases ledger 49,74
Sales ledger reports 78,79
Purchases ledger reports 75
Account balances

Task 78

Interpreting account balances

Objective

To obtain and interpret the account balances report (aged debtors' report).

Instructions

This printout gives details of the total amounts owed by each customer and of how old each part of the debt is. It is useful in credit control as it enables the business to quickly identify any customers who are slow in paying off their debts.

Activity

One account in the sales ledger that had a number of entries was the account for GEMFIT so it might be worthwhile to obtain a printout of the account history for this account. Select the option for ACCOUNT HISTORY from the SALES LEDGER REPORTS menu and enter GEMFIT as both lower and upper references.

```
DUDLEY TRADING PLC                      Sales Ledger Reports - Account History.


Account : GEMFIT   GEM FITTINGS PLC
-----------------------------------------------


No. Tp Date   Ref       Details           Value       Debit      Credit
---- -- ------ ------ -------------------- ---------- ---------- ----------
   5 SI 010987 O/bal  Opening balance      300.00      300.00
  25 SI 240987 Q127   TYPE AB              518.31 p
                      Amount Outstanding   318.31
  26 SI 240987 Q127   TYPE BB              437.00 p
                      Amount Outstanding   307.11
  27 SI 240987 Q127   TYPE DA              246.73 *   1202.04
  31 SC 280987 1891   TYPE BB              129.89                  129.89
  35 SR 231087 908765 Sales Receipt        500.00                  500.00

Amount Outstanding    :    872.15
Amount paid this period :    500.00
=================================================================================
```

Key words

Account history 22,23,66,76,77,79
Sales ledger reports 77,79
Aged account balances

Task 79

Examining account histories

Objective

To obtain and interpret the account history report for debtors.

Instructions

This printout shows that transaction no 5 has been paid off (it does not have an * next to it) and that transaction nos 25 and 26 have been part paid. Both of these transactions show the amount currently outstanding and the letter p signifies that they are only part paid. No 26 is marked as part paid because the credit note (no 31) has been matched with it.

The sales and purchase ledger should be integrated with the nominal ledger. This means that any transactions that are made in the sales or purchase ledger can be automatically entered in the nominal ledger. Check the nominal ledger to make sure that these items have been transferred.

Activity

Exit the sales ledger reports menu and select NOMINAL LEDGER REPORTS. When this menu appears select the option for ACCOUNT HISTORY. If you recall, it was stated earlier that when you entered discount in the account for WILKIN, the amount of the discount would be transferred automatically to the discount account in the nominal ledger. This can now be checked by examining the account history of the account for DISCOUNT — account no 0600. Type this in when the lower and upper account references are requested. This report can be directed to the screen as it should have just one entry.

```
DUDLEY TRADING PLC                    Nominal Ledger Reports - Account History.


Account : 0600     Discount
----------------------------------------------------


No. Tp Date   Ref    Details          Value      Debit      Credit
---- -- ------ ------ --------------------- ---------- ---------- ----------
 37 SC 021087 109902 Discount            20.30      20.30

                                      Totals  :     20.30      0.00
                                      Balance :     20.30
==================================================================================
```

Key words

Transaction 2,5,8,12,13,15,16,17,18,67,73,81
Debtors' account history
Nominal ledger reports
Accounts history 22,23,66,76,77,78
Discount 71,72
Sales ledger reports 77,78

Task 80 · Interpreting the discount account

Objective

To obtain and interpret the account history report for the discount account from the nominal ledger.

Instructions

The amount of the discount given was £20.30 so you should have the same screen as that shown in Task 79. This does not mention the account of WILKIN but the transaction does have the number 37. Type SC (sales credit) which should enable it to be traced in the audit trail.

Activity

Check also that details of the payments into and from the bank have been recorded by examining the bank account. However, the bank account is a CONTROL ACCOUNT and consequently you will have to select CONTROL ACCOUNTS from the menu if you want to confirm that all details have been entered.

A further check can be made by examining the DEBTOR'S CONTROL ACCOUNT; all entries which involve both sales and nominal ledgers should appear in this account. Select this option and you should get the following printout:

```
DUDLEY TRADING PLC                        Control Accounts - Debtor's Control.


Account : 0100     Debtor's Control
---------------------------------------------


    No. Tp  Date    Ref       Details        Value       Debit      Credit
    ---- --  ------  -----   ----------------  ----------  ---------- ----------
    19  SI  030987  0123    TYPE AA           403.08
    20  SI  030987  0123    TYPE DB           242.64      645.72
    21  SI  060987  0124    TYPE BA           633.31
    22  SI  060987  0124    TWINLOCKS         172.50      805.81
    23  SI  110987  0125    TYPE DA            87.11       87.11
    24  SI  180987  0126    PAPER              31.63       31.63
    25  SI  240987  0127    TYPE AB           518.31
    26  SI  240987  0127    TYPE BB           437.00
    27  SI  240987  0127    TYPE DA           246.73     1202.04
    28  SI  270987  0128    TYPES AA, AB     1384.08
    29  SI  270987  0128    TYPES DA, DB      518.99     1903.07
    30  SC  150987  1890    TYPE DB            66.24                   66.24
    31  SC  280987  1891    TYPE BB           129.89                  129.89
    34  SR  221087  435555  Sales Receipt     357.50                  357.50
    35  SR  231087  908765  Sales Receipt     500.00                  500.00
    36  SR  021087  109902  Sales Receipt     110.00
    37  SC  021087  109902  Discount           20.30                  130.30

                                          Totals  :     4675.38    1183.93
                                          Balance :     3491.45
    =============================================================================
```

Key words

Control accounts 5,17,23,24,25
Debtors' control account 81
Discount 71,72
Discount account

Task 81

Debtors' control account

Objective
To obtain and interpret the account history report for the debtors' control account.

Instructions
This printout shows all the original invoice and credit note details and also the details relating to payments received.

The final printout to consider is the options for the DAYBOOKS. These are generally only used to confirm details of any transaction and provide similar information to that shown in the audit trail except that they only list the details of the type requested.

Activity
Select the daybook for SALES INVOICES to obtain the following which lists details of all sales invoices *only*.

```
DUDLEY TRADING PLC                    Day Books - Sales Invoices.


No. Tp A/C    N/C    Date   Ref.    Details      Nett Am'nt Tax Am'nt Gross Amount  Tc
---- -- ----- ------ ------ ------  ----------   ---------- --------- -----------   --
  1 SI SMITH  0100   010987 O/bal  Opening balance  1000.00     0.00    1000.00     T9
  2 SI ABCLTD 0100   010987 O/bal  Opening balance   357.50     0.00     357.50     T9
  3 SI DCRLTD 0100   010987 O/bal  Opening balance   250.50     0.00     250.50     T9
  4 SI DOUGIE 0100   010987 O/bal  Opening balance   500.00     0.00     500.00     T9
  5 SI GEMFIT 0100   010987 O/bal  Opening balance   300.00     0.00     300.00     T9
  6 SI HUGHES 0100   010987 O/bal  Opening balance  1102.30     0.00    1102.30     T9
  7 SI ROMBOL 0100   010987 O/bal  Opening balance   450.00     0.00     450.00     T9
  8 SI WILKIN 0100   010987 O/bal  Opening balance   130.30     0.00     130.30     T9
 19 SI ABCLTD 1000   030987 Q123   TYPE AA          350.50    52.58     403.08     T1
 20 SI ABCLTD 1002   030987 Q123   TYPE DB          210.99    31.65     242.64     T1
 21 SI HUGHES 1001   060987 Q124   TYPE BA          550.70    82.61     633.31     T1
 22 SI HUGHES 1003   060987 Q124   TWINLOCKS        150.00    22.50     172.50     T1
 23 SI SMITH  1002   110987 Q125   TYPE DA           75.75    11.36      87.11     T1
 24 SI ROMBOL 1003   180987 Q126   PAPER             27.50     4.13      31.63     T1
 25 SI GEMFIT 1000   240987 Q127   TYPE AB          450.70    67.61     518.31     T1
 26 SI GEMFIT 1001   240987 Q127   TYPE BB          380.00    57.00     437.00     T1
 27 SI GEMFIT 1002   240987 Q127   TYPE DA          214.55    32.18     246.73     T1
 28 SI DCRLTD 1000   270987 Q128   TYPES AA, AB    1203.55   180.53    1384.08     T1
 29 SI DCRLTD 1002   270987 Q128   TYPES DA, DB     451.30    67.69     518.99     T1
                                                  ---------- --------- -----------
                                                    8156.14   609.84    8765.98
```

Key words
Daybook 24,63
Transaction 2,5,8,12,13,15,16,17,18,67,73,79
Debtors' control account 80

Final check
This concludes this series of lessons using SAGE. Not all reports and transactions have been examined but this is because most are so similar, for example the purchase invoices daybook and the sales invoices daybook. If you would like further practice then it is suggested that you continue examining the accounts in both the sales and purchase ledgers and clear all items, either by paying them off or giving discounts.

Index